"Most Christians are bored by or ignorant about 'missions.' If you include yourself in one of those categories, then put on your seat belt and get ready for the ride of your life. Drawing on his own experiences in some of the remotest places in the world, Joel Vestal tells a vivid and compelling story that will both challenge and reenergize how you think about Jesus' commission to disciple the nations today. As crucial as proclamation and evangelism are, Joel argues that the goal of missions should be 'whole-life transformational discipleship.' *Dangerous Faith* ought to come with a warning label: 'This book may drastically change your outlook on a world in need of Christ's love.'"

—WILLIAM W. KLEIN, PhD, professor of New Testament,
Denver Seminary

"There are so many stories of injustice, suffering, and pain in our world, and Joel Vestal has seen more of them at close range than most of us ever will. But there are even more stories of hope, joy, faith, commitment, love, and confidence going unreported in our world, and Joel captures dozens of those needed stories of good news in these pages. I was inspired to want to be a part of making more of those kinds of stories come true."

—BRIAN MCLAREN, pastor and author; anewkindofchristian.org

"Joel Vestal has earned the right to speak. His perspective on the struggles and successes of the global emerging church will greatly broaden you. His call toward wholeness and incarnation among the poor will find eager ears—mine included."

—ANDREW JONES, director, Boaz Project;
www.tallskinnykiwi.com

"*Dangerous Faith* will entertain and challenge you with faith stories of adventure and daring that provide insight into the difference one person can make in seeking to achieve God's call to a holistic mission. Joel Vestal took a step of faith at an early age and has continued to see God work in ways that will challenge and inspire. If you are searching for how you can make a difference, you will find practical help and inspiration in Joel Vestal's vision for the Whole Gospel, the Whole Person, and the Whole World."

—SAMUEL J. VOORHIES, PhD, director of leadership and
organizational development, World Vision International

"Joel has lived the whole gospel to the whole world better than most. That is why this book is not theory; it is authentic. Joel removes the walls that surround the western church and places us in the midst of the story of the whole church and lets us meet the real people who live out an amazing faith. This book is a must-read because it critiques the Christianity of those of us in the West and fuels our hearts to want more than what we are experiencing. The new face of mission must be holistic and look more like Jesus, and Joel explains why. If you are wanting more from your faith and wanting to enlarge your view of Jesus' global community, then you have to read this book!"

—RICK MCKINLEY, pastor, Imago Dei Community; author of *Jesus in the Margins* and *Finding God in the Places We Ignore*

"When Joel has something to say, I eagerly listen. Reading this book is like reading a thrilling mission adventure combined with theological challenge. *Dangerous Faith* will not only help redefine mission for the church but will also help ignite your heart about what it means to be a follower of Jesus."

—DAN KIMBALL, author of *The Emerging Church* and pastor of Vintage Faith Church, Santa Cruz, California

"There are many people telling us how the Christian mission is changing. But if you want to know what this change looks like from the inside, I can't think of a better place to look than Joel Vestal's new book. It gives glimpses of the exciting new world of missions that I have not seen anywhere else."

—WILLIAM A. DYRNESS, PhD, professor of Theology and Culture, Fuller Theological Seminary, Pasadena, California

"Joel Vestal represents a fresh, new vision of missions spreading among global Christianity's younger generation that is decidedly personal, yet universal; warmly evangelical, yet socially engaged; local in perspective, yet globally aware — managing to effectively bridge many characteristics that have divided Christians in the past. The reader will be challenged to integrate many seemingly disparate streams of commitment into a global Christian worldview."

—TODD M. JOHNSON, PhD, director, Center for the Study of Global Christianity, Gordon-Conwell Theological Seminary, Boston, Massachusetts

To see what others are saying about *Dangerous Faith*, please visit www.servlife.org.

NAVPRESS DELIBERATE

From the very beginning, God created humans to love Him and each other. He intended for His people to be a blessing to everyone on earth so that everyone would know Him (see Genesis 12:2). Jesus also taught this over and over and promised to give His people all they needed to make it happen—His resources, His power, and His presence (see Matthew 28:20; John 14:12-14). NavPress Deliberate takes Him at His word and stirs its readers to do the same—to be the children of God for whom creation is groaning to be revealed. We have only to glance through the Bible to discover what it looks like to be the blessing God has intended: caring for the poor, orphan, widow, prisoner, and foreigner (see Micah 6:8; Matthew 25:31-46; Isaiah 58); and redeeming the world—everyone and everything in it (see Colossians 1:19-20; Romans 8:19-23).

NavPress Deliberate encourages readers to embrace this holistic and vibrant Christian faith: It is both contemplative and active; it unites mystery-embracing faith with theological rootedness; it breaks down the sacred/secular divide, recognizing God's sovereignty and redemptive work in every facet of life; it dialogues with other faiths and worldviews and embraces God's truth found there; it creates culture and uses artistic ability to unflinchingly tell the truth about this life and God's redemption of it; it fosters a faith bold enough to incarnate the gospel in a shrinking and diverse world. NavPress Deliberate is for everyone on a pilgrimage to become like Jesus and to continue His work of living and discipling among all people.

Become what you believe.

The NavPress Deliberate Team

Joel Vestal

DANGEROUS FAITH

Growing in God and Service to the World

NAVPRESS

The Navigators is an international Christian organization. Our mission is to advance the gospel of Jesus and His kingdom into the nations through spiritual generations of laborers living and discipling among the lost. We see a vital movement of the gospel, fueled by prevailing prayer, flowing freely through relational networks and out into the nations where workers for the kingdom are next door to everywhere.

NavPress is the publishing ministry of The Navigators. The mission of NavPress is to reach, disciple, and equip people to know Christ and make Him known by publishing life-related materials that are biblically rooted and culturally relevant. Our vision is to stimulate spiritual transformation through every product we publish.

© 2007 by Joel Keith Vestal

All rights reserved. No part of this publication may be reproduced in any form without written permission from NavPress, P.O. Box 35001, Colorado Springs, CO 80935.
www.navpress.com

NAVPRESS, BRINGING TRUTH TO LIFE, and the NAVPRESS logo are registered trademarks of NavPress. Absence of ® in connection with marks of NavPress or other parties does not indicate an absence of registration of those marks.

ISBN-13: 978-1-60006-197-4
ISBN-10: 1-60006-197-4

Cover design by The DesignWorks Group, Charles Brock, www.thedesignworksgroup.com
Cover photos by Getty and Shutterstock
Creative Team: Caleb Seeling, Keith Wall, Arvid Wallen, Pat Reinheimer, Kathy Guist

Some of the anecdotal illustrations in this book are true to life and are included with the permission of the persons involved. All other illustrations are composites of real situations, and any resemblance to people living or dead is coincidental.

Unless otherwise identified, all Scripture quotations in this publication are taken from the HOLY BIBLE: NEW INTERNATIONAL VERSION® (NIV®). Copyright © 1973, 1978, 1984 by International Bible Society. Used by permission of Zondervan Publishing House. All rights reserved. Also used is the *King James Version* (KJV); and *THE MESSAGE* (MSG). Copyright © 1993, 1994, 1995, 1996, 2000, 2001, 2002, 2005. Used by permission of NavPress Publishing Group. The author's paraphrases are marked PAR.

Vestal, Joel, 1972-
  Dangerous faith : growing in God and service to the world / Joel Vestal.
     p. cm.
  Rev. ed. of: Wanting more.
  Includes bibliographical references.
  ISBN-13: 978-1-60006-197-4
  ISBN-10: 1-60006-197-4
  1. Christian life. I. Vestal, Joel, 1972- Wanting more. II. Title.
BV4501.3.V47 2007
248.4--dc22
                              2007020945
Printed in the United States of America

1 2 3 4 5 6 7 8 / 11 10 09 08 07

To the Anjali Biswakarmas of the world

CONTENTS

FOREWORD

A few things were crystal clear to me the very first time I met Joel Vestal. For one, I knew right away that he cared deeply about the people of the world and was burdened about the injustice, poverty, and spiritual darkness that are a way of life for so many. I also knew in that first encounter that Joel wasn't waiting for permission from anybody to do something to help them, especially given the fact that Jesus had already entrusted to him the mission of communicating His love and kindness to them in tangible ways.

Our first meeting occurred when Joel was just a college freshman. But he was already a man with a purpose that encompassed the nations.

While a lot of other students were innocently immersed in conversations about their social lives (or lack thereof) or some hot cultural topic, Joel was talking about unreached people groups and ways to connect them to God's redemption story. And he wasn't just reciting statistics and spouting off information; his heart was pulsing with compassion and an urgency to act — now. Before long, Joel had forged an alliance with a pastor in a remote region of India where few others dared to go and the gospel was seldom, if ever, heard.

To be completely honest, at first glance I thought Joel was a little overzealous and had a lot to learn. But over time my reservation morphed into admiration and respect, as the little seed he planted in Bihar, India, sprouted to become ServLife International, the fruit of a solitary student emboldened by the Spirit of God and determined to leverage his life so that people all over the world could hear the name of Jesus Christ.

It's staggering to think just how many people on the planet have never heard of Jesus, much less any of His life-giving words. Like us, they wonder about the meaning of life and long to know their maker. Yet they have never heard of Jesus Christ—the unique Son of God come to earth, the Divine in human flesh, the Father's gracious sacrifice for all our sins.

And we're not just talking about a handful of people in some remote village deep in the Amazon jungle. We're talking about hundreds of millions without Christ, dotting every continent on earth. Most are clustered in central Asia, where China and India comprise more than half of the world's population. That's why it is no surprise that right smack in the middle of that region, in a town in northern India near the Nepalese border, Joel first raised the ServLife banner, announcing the kingdom of God.

Yet equally staggering is the number of us who *have* heard of Jesus Christ—and call Him Savior—and have still failed to take seriously His last words to us. Recorded at the close of the gospels of Matthew and Mark and in the first chapter of the book of Acts, Christ's words propel us outward with a clear mandate to take His story to every person on earth (see Matthew 28:18-20; Mark 16:15; Acts 1:8).

I don't think Jesus was implying that we all should be "missionaries" in the traditional western sense of that word; rather, we should lead "mission lifestyles," being concerned about the well-being of all people and creatively using our gifts and means to bring them hope now and the message of life that never ends.

While people in every generation have eagerly and sacrificially answered that call, I'm encouraged to see a new wave of young people emerge with a passion to amplify God's fame among the nations at all cost. I think you'll be inspired (and convicted) to join them after reading the pages that follow — and not out of a sense of guilt, but as the natural overflow of what God has so generously lavished on us.

As you go, Joel and his wife, Elise, will be right there with you, blazing a trail with their words and actions, compelling countless others to follow — myself included.

At the end of the day, this God-mission to preach good news and bring restoration to every man, woman, and child will succeed, ushering in the end of life as we know it and the coming Christ. I want to be standing (kneeling) in that moment, knowing that my life's influence extended past the edge of the subdivision and beyond the halls of the office. I want to be able to eternally rejoice, knowing that God allowed me to play a role in gathering every tribe and tongue to proclaim His praise. I think in that moment, everything else in life will pale in comparison to that reward.

Louie Giglio
founder, Passion Conferences
www.268generation.com

ACKNOWLEDGMENTS

First, I wish to thank my wife, Jill Elise. Your love, support, and encouragement mean more than you know. To my son, Zayd: You have been my little inspiration as we dragged you to the Himalayas, the beaches of Thailand, the tallest building in the world in Kuala Lumpur, and the villages in India—all before you turned one. You will be the envy of all your future classmates when it is "show and tell" day! To my beautiful daughter, Daya: You bring joy to my heart every time I look into your eyes.

Thank you to all ServLife staff members who are doing justice and loving mercy and walking humbly before God in many difficult areas of the world.

And, ultimately, my thanks belongs to the One who is the giver of all good things: the Lord Jesus Christ.

DO WHAT OTHERS CAN'T OR WON'T

Dangerous faith is living a life of obedience to Jesus and not worrying about the consequences. It is a holistic faith that is about bending every aspect of our lives—every daily routine, every unusual circumstance—to glorify God, even to the point of risking our very lives. After all, God is less concerned about our safety than He is about receiving glory through our lives. And our lives are like a web of many connecting strands; just as there are many organs in a human body, which all must be active and connected to make the whole body work, so are we as individuals in our relationship with God.

Often the church has separated the different parts of our Christian faith and made us think that our prayer and devotional life have nothing to do with how we live in community with the world. How does our worship of God impact our understanding of persecution and suffering? How is our personal relationship with Him directly connected to the ways we choose to demonstrate love to our neighbors, including those neighbors who live halfway around the globe?

Augustine wrote that the older we grow in faith, the less we like to be instructed—but we all need to be reminded. This book will take you on a journey across the globe and, at the same time, remind you of some important keys for your own spiritual journey at home. Perhaps it will bring instruction for some as well. My hope is that it will leave you ready to risk, step out in faith, and live the adventure called Christianity. You don't have to buy a plane ticket or get your passport to travel with me (though perhaps you will want to by the time you've finished reading). But I wish to take you to far-off corners of the world and share with you different experiences and encounters that have shaped me and helped me to know more of God and the world we live in. I wish to share with you how God has transformed me, and I pray that through reading this book you will allow God to transform you as well. This book is part autobiography, part spiritual formation manual, and part mission book. But it is all written out of love and a desire to see God's kingdom expanded across the world.

I am in debt to countless people, both living and dead, who have helped mold me and teach me what it means to follow Jesus Christ. The ideas expressed in this book have come through conversations, encounters with people, many books, the stories shared by others, and the experiences God has blessed me to have throughout the world.

If there are two hopes I have for any reader of this book, young or old, they are these: First, I hope you will seize the opportunity to travel and see your life, faith, and the kingdom of God from different ethnic, economic, and political perspectives than your own. There is an African proverb that says, "He who does not travel thinks his mother is the best cook. But the one who travels knows his mother is among other good cooks." The diversity of thoughts, colors, tastes, rituals, and cultures in the world could have been created only by the greatest artist of all time, our Creator. I believe that if we do not build global community, heaven is going to be a shock for many of us. I encourage you to seek out global community for yourself, your family, and your local church.

My second hope, which is even greater than the first, is that your hunger for God will awaken and grow beyond your wildest imagination. I hope you will want more of God—want to know Him, hunger for Him, and glorify Him. There are many views on where to find God. As Christians, we first look to Jesus Christ, the living Word, and to Scripture to come to know God. However, I believe there are many places—perhaps even unlikely places—where you can meet God: standing in an art gallery, watching a film, looking at an old photograph, being among the poor, exploring nature, experiencing the death of someone close to you, getting married, becoming a parent, or developing a close friendship.

People spend their whole lives seeking, searching, and wanting to connect with their Maker. You cannot grow in this pursuit unless you hunger for it. You cannot hunger for it unless your appetite is aroused. I pray that through this book your appetite will be awakened to pursue loving God with all of your mind, soul, and strength while you love your neighbor as yourself. In the words of Jim Elliot, "Don't give yourselves to what others can do but will not do, but give yourselves to what others cannot do and will not do!"

chapter one

THE BRIDE IS BIGGER THAN YOU THINK

*Kingdom people seek first the kingdom of God and its justice;
church people often put church work above concerns of
justice, mercy, and truth. Church people think about how to
get people into the church; kingdom people think about how
to get the church into the world. Church people worry that
the world might change the church; kingdom people work to
see the church change the world.*

HOWARD SNYDER

*Just as one could not speak of the church without speaking of
its mission, it was impossible to think of the church without
thinking, in the same breath, of the world to which it is sent.*

DAVID BOSCH

*The church is both the goal and the agent of world
evangelization. Mission disengagement from the church is a
biblical oxymoron.*

FRANK SEVERN

We left the capital of Kampala, Uganda, on a small prop plane to visit the refugees from Sudan who fled the civil war that had been raging in their homeland for decades. Since this was my first time in the Sudan region, I was on the edge of my seat with anticipation. I could not imagine a region that war had ravaged for decades—killing millions and displacing millions more.

Once on the plane, I quickly realized I was the only foreigner there. After we took off, an African man looked at me with a perplexed expression and asked, "Where are you going?"

I told him I was flying to the refugee camps of Adjumani.

He responded quickly, "Don't you know that the American embassy has banned Americans from traveling to this region?"

Fear immediately welled up in my belly, and I envisioned my mug shot on the front page of the newspaper, accompanied by the headline, "American murdered in Uganda." I told the man that I did not know that, but I was traveling with Sudanese friends and was trusting God to protect us. I explained that we were going to help the refugees in their struggle to merely survive. The man responded with a smile and thanked me for having the courage to go.

My Sudanese friend kept telling me he did not know how we would get to our destination, a village about thirty miles from the dirt-and-grass airstrip where we would land. He was taking me to the community he had first gone to when he fled Sudan. Not long after his arrival at that camp, he had started a church.

"Are there any taxis at the airport where we'll be landing?" I asked him.

"No," he said. "There are no taxis, but God will lead us."

"What about buses that might take us to the camp?" I asked.

"No buses," he said, "but God will lead us."

I was beginning to imagine us walking for hours. *What if we get stuck in the middle of the bush in Africa? What if the local LRA (Ugandan rebels) attacked us?* Once again, panic welled within me. I began to pray, and I opened up the Scriptures for guidance. I remembered what God said to Joshua: "Have I not commanded you? Be strong and courageous. Do not be terrified; do not be discouraged, for the LORD your

God will be with you wherever you go" (Joshua 1:9). For a moment, calm overtook my anxiety.

When we landed, there were only about a half dozen vehicles in sight, all belonging to nongovernment organizations. The people quickly filed off the plane, got into the waiting vehicles, and sped away. Then the African man who had spoken with me on the plane approached and asked, "Do you need a ride to Adjumani? I will take you and your friend."

After a group of us helped push the plane out of the mud, we all loaded up and headed off on the dirt roads to our destination. The lush greenery was overwhelming. We soon approached a river, and I realized there was no bridge to take us across.

One of our escorts told me, "We have come to the Nile, but the ferry workers are not working today, so we must cross by canoe."

The famed Nile River! It was so mighty and beautiful I could hardly pull my gaze from it. I had seen the Nile once before in Cairo, but seeing it farther south was astonishing.

We all waited, and before long, two African men in a small dugout canoe came rowing up to the shore. The canoe was so small that I

The Nile

Waiting to Cross the Nile

really didn't think it could keep us all afloat. Without many other options, I climbed in. A man handed me my duffel bag. And then a tied-up calf to place beside me. And then a small bicycle. Pretty soon I couldn't move an inch. The water came right to the edge of our little canoe, and I strongly suspected I was about to go *swimming* down the Nile. I was certain the baby cow next to me would start kicking at any moment.

Despite my dire predictions, the canoe stayed afloat, the calf behaved, and we eventually made it across the Nile without incident. And a few hours later, we finally arrived at Adjumani. The villagers were all present to greet us with singing and dancing. We watched as one group at a time began worshiping God by singing as they marched into the small church, which was made of mud and grass. First the children strode enthusiastically into the church. They were followed by several other groups, the last of which was composed of the church elders and older adults. Finally it was my turn to go in, but I quickly found I couldn't enter the building to hear the instruments and sing-ing—there was simply no room!

I truly have to say that the unmistakable and indescribable joy on the faces of the refugees gave me a taste of what heaven must be like. The children were all running around half-naked, with bloated stomachs and smiling faces. After the service, I talked with the local pastor, and at one point I asked what the average offering was. He told me it was less than one U.S. dollar.

So there we were, in the middle of a refugee camp with a local church of about two hundred and fifty individuals. These people would probably never possess the means to travel throughout Africa or other parts of the world. Most were malnourished and lived on United Nations handouts. But there was something transcendent that captured me in this local church, and it was the obvious, and almost palpable, hunger and love for God.

As I was leaving the church after spending most of the day there, I noticed a sign nailed to a tree. It read, "Adjumani Church: The Center for Global Impact and World Evangelization."

This was a church with meager resources. The members were all refugees, most of whom would probably never leave their village. But they possessed something that is close to the heart of God: a passion and vision for all the world to know the Savior. Now that's a model churches everywhere should emulate. There in that poor, ramshackle village was a group of believers who looked upon their congregation as "the center" for global impact and world evangelism. And who's to say that it wasn't?

In America, it's common to drive by a church building and say, "Wow, look at that church!" Yes, that is a church building, but it is not *the church*. The church is made up of people. Bricks and mortar and stained glass have little to do with what makes the church what God intended it to be. I preached my first sermon at a church when I was sixteen years old while standing under a tree in Malawi, Africa. Some

Sermon Tree

may insist that it wasn't really a church but a "preaching point" or "outreach post." To me, that certainly *was* a church, and on that particular day it met under a tree. They saw themselves as the body of Christ in that place.

THE GROWTH OF THE CHURCH

The church has grown more in the twentieth century than in all centuries since the time of Christ combined, with almost two billion adherents worldwide.[1] The current number of 81 million believers in China is expected to swell to 135 million by 2025. The 50 million faithful in India could mushroom to 125 million by 2050. And today's census of 90 million Christians in Africa is likely to explode to 1 billion by 2050.[2]

Today around the world, there are:

- 3.45 million churches — only 8 percent of these in North America
- 33,800 Christian denominations
- 23,000 parachurch or service organizations
- 4,100 foreign mission sending organizations
- 1 million full-time ordained clergy (8 percent women)[3]

For those who think that we as Americans are the only laborers left to fulfill the Great Commission of our Lord, these statistics are both humbling and encouraging. We must explore new methods and models of partnering, collaborating, and converging with our brothers and sisters in other nations to reach the lost across the globe.

THE "INDIGENOUS" ADVANTAGE

We decided to go on a two-day rafting trip in Nepal for a mere eight dollars. "How could we pass this up?" I asked my friend. We were young, eager for adventure, and on a limited budget, so this was definitely our kind of trip, especially since it included all food, camping gear, transportation, and guides. After arriving at the Trisuli River, we set off for hours of soaking in the beauty of the Himalayas. It was my first time rafting, and I was beyond thrilled.

A few hours into the journey, we came upon a big rock that

After Our Rafting Adventure

capsized our raft and plunged us into the water. At first I didn't mind—I was ready to go swimming. However, the water was more powerful than it looked. After splashing and struggling for a while, I finally found the raft. Relieved as I was for my own safety, I was desperately concerned about my Indian friend, Albert. After all, Albert didn't know how to swim. We had tried to talk him out of going with us, but he was determined to share in the adventure, so we had acquiesced.

As it turned out, Albert made it through the mishap all right, but he reacted to the experience quite differently than the rest of us. Later that evening, several of us were sitting around the campfire discussing what had happened and thanking God for protecting us. Albert, meanwhile, was off to the side talking with four Nepalis, all of them seated together inside a raft. Some time later, I asked Albert what they talked about, and he told me the four men came from the mountain villages and spoke a language he had never heard before. They were Newari and came from a low caste. There are over seventy languages and dialects spoken in Nepal, and many of them overlap. Albert spoke several languages himself, including English, Nepali, Hindi, Bengali, and Bhojpuri.

"I figured out their language as we were talking, and I began to tell them about the gospel," Albert explained. "They had never heard of Jesus Christ before. I told them how I almost died in the river but that my God saved me and takes care of His children. They were amazed that I would even talk to them because I come from a higher caste."

What astonished me about Albert's story was that it took him only minutes to communicate the gospel to these men in their own language—in a way a westerner most likely could never have done. My view of world evangelization shifted that evening by the campfire.

I grew up my whole life hearing how America was going to "win the world to Christ." Perhaps it was not said exactly like this, but the idea was certainly strongly communicated in the way missions were talked about and done. Of course, I'm speaking of my particular childhood denomination, but others no doubt conveyed the same message. We as the church in the West have been guilty of thinking that *we* will evangelize the world using our big budgets, large programs, and great strategic ideas. To this day, the church in America still approaches missions with a blatantly western idealism and a business model of international mission work. We analyze the "markets." We sell our "good and services." As James Engel and William Dyrness point out, "this western and contemporary missions' understanding is too often captive to American cultural realities, associating the gospel with economic and political pragmatism."[4]

Many Americans still say things like, "Don't invest in indigenous workers; they may steal your money." Or, "Nationals can't do it without our western technology and techniques." Or, "The nationals are not trained well enough to be able to reach their own people for Christ."

Well, we might want to mention China to people who think like this! China's unregistered church has hardly been touched by the West, yet it has grown tremendously without our technology, money, or training. The way the world is going to be evangelized is through the *whole church* — not just the American church — taking the whole gospel to the whole person all around the world.

Clearly, the way we approach global ministry in North America needs to expand. Webster's defines the word *paradox* as "a statement that is seemingly contradictory or opposed to common sense, and yet is perhaps true."[5] Maybe it is a paradox to say that we as westerners can make the most impact overseas by taking a backseat and working through local church communities indigenous to a particular region. After all, these people know their culture and language. They live by the same standard of living and face the same daily struggles as the people they are trying to reach.

Once I visited a western missionary in India, and he told me he had to return to the U.S. because his kids did not like the Indian culture, and family problems had arisen. I know God used this missionary family, but their story caused me to lament over the huge amount of resources and energy it took to place an American family like theirs on the mission field, even though we know the rate of long-term service is relatively low. It is estimated that it costs about $100,000 each year for a missionary family to be on the mission field overseas. It does not sadden me that westerners go overseas, but it does sadden me when I hear stories of how their work is forced to stop because of cultural problems, political unrest, or personal problems. I know this is not the case for all western missionaries. Many do an excellent job of working themselves out of a job by empowering the indigenous community. Yet the simple fact is that indigenous missionaries do not leave their homes if a civil conflict breaks out or if they have family problems. Why? Because their mission field *is their home.*

Am I saying that western missionaries should not go into the world? Absolutely not! It is crucial to the way we understand and live the gospel that we send our own "sons and daughters" into the world to share the good news. The Great Commission is a command for *all* Christians throughout the world, no matter how large or small their church is or what country they call home. In fact, my family and I live in Nepal as I write this book, so how could I advocate that western missionaries are not called and sent around the world? I believe that we as the western church do play a crucial role in world evangelization. Yet the western church simply cannot accomplish the task on its own.

For example, I recently read that thirty American Peace Corps volunteers in Nepal were forced to leave their district following an ultimatum by an armed group of Maoists. The Maoists, who hold a negative attitude toward Americans, demanded that the volunteers leave their region within six days. But even if the Americans had been allowed to stay for the present, they would still have to leave eventually. In Nepal, expatriates are allowed to stay in the country for only ten years and may not stay beyond the age of sixty-five. With this reality, which is similar to so many other places in the world, we simply cannot "go it alone" as westerners in our efforts to reach the world for Christ. To genuinely fulfill the Great Commission, we have no choice but to work with and through local believers to plant churches and minister to the poor and marginalized. Of course, I realize that such cooperative relationships are not always possible, especially in unreached communities or cities where very few, if any, Christians live. But in general, interdependence is healthy in cross-cultural mission work—in whatever way that is expressed. To carry out the Great Commission effectively, we need interdependent relationships with other believers around the world just as surely as we need the power of the Holy Spirit.

In 1997, several partners and I started a children's home and orphanage in north India. It is still in operation and is run by indigenous staff. The region of India where the home is located is very hostile to Christians, even if they are Indian. One local Hindu man

A Children's Home Is Born in North India

often sent his own child plus a few other children to throw rocks at the orphans every evening as they gathered to sing worship songs.

After doing this for several months, the Hindu man approached our Indian director and said, "I have noticed that you have come here and that you are an educated man. I was surprised by your presence here and did not understand why you came to this poor place. However, I see that you walk everywhere you go, and therefore I am convinced that you are a holy man. I was sending my son to throw the stones at your children singing to your God, but I now want to send him to be a part of your day-school program."

You see, in India when a person walks everywhere he goes, he is revered and respected as a holy man. All Hindu priests and Sadhus (Hindu holy men) walk wherever they go.

By contrast, if I lived in this region, I would want to have an SUV and all the things that I thought I needed to reach these people for Christ. But when you work through the indigenous communities, you work according to their culture and customs. Of course, western missionaries can adjust and adapt to different aspects of the culture they are living and working in. But if I have to choose between having someone local preaching the gospel or a foreigner preaching the gospel, I will always choose the indigenous person, even if the foreigner is a "better" preacher. Why? Because in most of the regions of the world where the gospel has not taken root and grown, the vast majority of the people perceive Christianity as a "white man's" religion that is of interest only to westerners. To work apart from the indigenous church in any area of the world is simply not the wisest thing to do.

Of course, if there are no indigenous believers in a particular region, or if their numbers are very small, you may have to go it alone for a time or else work in cooperation with Christians in a neighboring region or country where the Christian population is larger. But wherever it is possible, I believe that partnering directly with the indigenous church is the most effective way to further the gospel.

ServLife India Conference

Some might respond by saying, "We can't work with the indigenous church because they do not believe the right thing or do the right things like they need to." My response is simple: How often does God look at us as His children and say, "You do not do the right thing or believe the right thing, but I still work through you." God is patient with us and does not give up on us. We must adopt the same attitude with all of God's children across the globe.

In Paul's letter to the church in Colossae, he mentions his friend Tychicus and calls him a "fellow servant in the Lord" (Colossians 4:7). The Greek term translated "fellow servant" in this passage is *sundoulos*, which means "a co-slave—a servitor or ministrant of the same master."[6] Paul is saying that he is equal to this man as a fellow slave of the same master. So we are to other followers of Jesus Christ. We are co-slaves of Christ, laboring together to see God's kingdom come and God's will be done on earth as it is in heaven.

THE FRUIT OF THE CHURCH

I remember going to Korea for the first time while I was in college. For any follower of Jesus, seeing the fervency of the Korean church in prayer is a humbling experience. The older airport in Seoul is close to the heart of the city, and when you fly in at night, you can see the city covered with little red neon crosses on the tops of the buildings. These crosses mark where either small groups of believers or large churches meet to worship. The red symbolizes the blood of Christ covering the city. It is an amazing sight. Today, South Korea is the second most sending nation in the world when it comes to missions—second only to the United States. In 1979, there were only about seventy-nine missionaries from Korea, but today there is an estimated twelve thousand.

One South Korean missionary commented, "There is a saying that when Koreans now arrive in a new place, they establish a church; the Chinese establish a restaurant; the Japanese, a factory."[7] The largest Methodist, Presbyterian, and Assembly of God churches are located in South Korea. The largest church in the world is in Seoul: Yoido Full Gospel Church. With all the satellite campuses, it is estimated to be more than 800,000 people strong. In the main building alone, more than 100,000 gather every weekend to worship God.

As you look at the amazing growth of the church in places like Korea, there is great reason to rejoice. But there is also a need to ask ourselves some important questions. One of the most important is, "What is the church producing?" Are we really producing disciples as Jesus instructed us to do? As Dallas Willard asked, "Have we inserted an omission in the Great Commission?"[8]—meaning, are we actually making disciples as Jesus commanded us to do in Matthew 28:19-20, or are we making something else?

In Rwanda in the early nineties, a horrific genocide occurred in which 800,000 people were killed. If you researched Rwanda, you would see that at the time of this travesty, the nation was statistically over 80 percent Christian. If that 80 percent had truly been trained and nurtured to become mature disciples of Jesus, perhaps the terrible genocide could have been avoided. Even today, some mission organizations don't consider Rwanda in their strategic planning because they say the country already has such a high percentage of professing Christians. But have those Christians received the discipleship training they need to become mature, effective followers of Christ?

The central issue, as I see it, is that our missionary efforts should not be reduced solely to proclamation and evangelism; instead they should focus on whole-life transformational discipleship. After all, we are not commanded to make *converts*; we are commanded to make *disciples*. As one African Christian leader said to a group of western missionaries, "You missionaries brought us Christ but never taught us how to live."[9]

In order for transformational discipleship to happen, much of the church around the world needs encouragement and training. That training can come from many different places, not just the western church. Churches in every culture around the world share at least one important question in common: Is it more important to fill up your church or to equip your people to leave your church for ministry? From the perspective of many western churches, the easy answer will always be "both." But if you look at our western churches' priorities—how the money is spent or decisions are made—you will usually discover that the reality is different from what we say. Surely the mistake the church has made is that it focuses more on getting people inside the four walls and meeting their "needs" rather than equipping them for ministry out in the world.

Author Brian McLaren says,

In my thinking, church doesn't exist for the benefit of its members. It exists to equip its members for the benefit of the world. . . . We don't recruit people to be customers of our products or consumers of our religious programs; we recruit them to be colleagues in our mission. The church doesn't exist to satisfy the consumer demands of believers; the church exists to equip and mobilize men and women for God's mission in the world.[10]

Indeed, the mission of the church must include *both* introducing the gospel to people and growing people in the gospel. Both tasks are equally important. But both are rarely done.

In the teaching I do with untrained pastors in developing countries, I often address this issue and ask them which task they believe is the most important. I will often have them raise their hands to indicate their choice. Most of the time they do not know how to respond, thinking it is an "either/or" answer. I then tell the following story to illustrate the need within the church to do both:

There was once a wise old teacher who held up a glass of water and asked his young pupil the age-old question, "What do you see? Is the glass half full or half empty?"

The pupil said to his teacher, "It depends whether you are filling it up or pouring it out to empty it."

"Well, what are you doing the most?" the teacher asked.

The pupil responded, "I believe I am constantly doing both."

The wise teacher replied, "It has been revealed to you the purpose of the glass!"

Filling up and pouring out—both are essential to the effectiveness of churches everywhere. It is the gathering of people for worship, sacrament, teaching, and community so that they can be sent out to demonstrate and proclaim the love of God in their community and the entire world. Unfortunately, churches in the West are usually best known for the first aspect (bringing people in) but rarely for the second (sending disciples out). You can probably name several churches in your area that are great at *filling up* their sanctuaries but not so great at *pouring out* their members into the world. This simply should not be! Every church's vision should carry global implications, because God always has a global agenda and vision.

Actively participating in God's global purposes is something every church should do, right from the very first day of its existence. This is not only wise but also good theology, as God is a "missionary God" who desires worshipers from all nations and tribes. Acts 1:8 clearly states that outreach and ministry from a local church should simultaneously target our own city (Jerusalem), our local region (Judea), the larger region (Samaria), and other areas across the globe (the ends of the earth).

THE GOSPEL AND LIFE TRANSFORMATION

Once, while in Africa, I had the opportunity to talk to an African Bible scholar and missionary. He said to me, "Many Christian leaders and Bible scholars in the western world have made a great mistake by separating everything in the Christian life. If you want to know a cat, you don't cut up the cat and study its different parts in separate pieces. Instead you live with the cat and come to know it."

Many surveys have been done to describe how there is not much difference between church people and nonchurch people in the West when it comes to giving to the poor, divorce rate, and honesty in business affairs. Why do you suppose that is?

The word *disciple* is used almost three hundred times in the Bible. The word *Christian* is used three times. Should this tell us something? Has the church been more concerned about "decisions" and "converts" than about making people authentic followers of Jesus, committed to live as "students" of Jesus their entire lives? The philosopher Søren Kierkegaard pointed out that the church is filled with "the admirers of Jesus" but not many followers. For too long we have allowed ourselves to be satisfied with churches full of people who are merely cultural

Christians or admirers of Jesus and have never had their lives transformed by the power of the gospel. Being a follower of Jesus means that we are transformed into His likeness. The apostle Paul said,

> *Whenever anyone turns to the Lord, the veil is taken away. Now the Lord is the Spirit, and where the Spirit of the Lord is, there is freedom. And we, who with unveiled faces all reflect the Lord's glory, are being transformed into his likeness with ever-increasing glory, which comes from the Lord, who is the Spirit. (2 Corinthians 3:16-18)*

The goal of Christian discipleship is not *information* but *transformation*. To be transformed means to change in character, form, or appearance. This is what the gospel does to us. It changes us. I am not talking about mere external changes, such as the style of clothing we wear, our tastes in the arts, or the way we talk. The gospel changes our very soul so our motives, attitudes, and intentions come to reflect Jesus Christ to the world.

I like what Rick Warren writes about this:

> *God's ultimate goal for your life on earth is not comfort, but character development. He wants you to grow up spiritually and become like Christ. Becoming like Christ does not mean losing your personality or becoming a mindless clone. God created your uniqueness, so he certainly does not want to destroy it. Christlikeness is all about transforming your character, not your personality.*[11]

The father of the Indian Constitution, Dr. B. R. Ambedkar, was at one time interested in embracing Christ. In 1956, he was asked, "Which religion does not oppress people?" The question inspired him to find an answer. He studied Hinduism, Buddhism, and Christianity and came to the conclusion that Christianity was the only one that taught equality. He was ready to embrace the teachings of Jesus, but the day he went to a church, he found two communion stations. He asked a leader in the church, "Why are there two communion stations?"

The church leader responded, "One is for the high caste and the other for the low caste."

Dr. Ambedkar was greatly disturbed by this and eventually decided to embrace Buddhism instead. What a lost opportunity for the gospel in India!

Even the great Mahatma Gandhi was once kicked out of a church in England while he was there pursuing his studies. He responded to the affront by saying, "I thought Christianity teaches love. This is not love."

Oftentimes the church does not display or teach the true message of Christ: equality and love. The reality is that the church today is filled with people who have not been transformed into the image of Jesus Christ but are merely going through religious ritual.

Perhaps the root of the problem is that we have made the gospel too easy or too comfortable for too long for too many people in the church. We have allowed people to hear the gospel over and over in comfortable complacency with no visible progression toward transformation. Yes, we are patient with people, but perhaps we are too tolerant of those who do not really want to follow Jesus Christ with their whole lives. Gordon Cosby of the Church of the Savior in Washington, DC, says,

We must come to the place where we can do what Jesus did, where we can watch the rich young ruler walk away and, with sorrow and an ache in our hearts, let him go until he can come back on the terms of Jesus Christ. We have been so afraid we might lose potential members that we have been willing to take them on their own terms. Then we wonder why the church is relatively impotent and doesn't have the power to transform human life, to shake society to its very roots.[12]

WHO CARES ABOUT THE STRUCTURE?

When should an adjective be inserted before the word *church* to define who or what the church is? I think we should be careful about using adjectives to define our churches. So many want to define their church by inserting *house, seeker, postmodern, mega,* or *organic* before the word *church* to broadcast the church's style or structure to the world. Of course, I understand that descriptive words are sometimes needed to distinguish between the different models and ways of various churches. But very often these words serve only to distract believers from God's core purpose for the church. We get so busy *being* postmodern or mega or seeker that we forget our true goal: *becoming* like Jesus and sharing His message of love with the world.

These descriptive labels can also tend to foster division between different churches in a community or region. Many who use these "defining adjectives" make the bold claim that their particular form or structure for the church is the "best" or "only" way church can be done. But the church is more than any one structure or any one particular style. The word *church* comes from the Greek word *ecclesia*, and its meaning is broad and simple: "calling out, i.e. (concretely) a popular meeting, especially a religious congregation."[13] There is room for great diversity and multiple models within the body of Christ. In fact, such diversity is essential if we are to reach the world for Christ. Churches that meet in houses, five-hundred-year-old cathedrals, or modern school cafeterias are all valid. Churches that enjoy pipe organs, electric guitars, or a sitar should all exist. Some churches may choose to gather large crowds of people and create smaller groups out of that, while others emphasize only the small groups themselves. The core issues of a healthy, vibrant church are rooted not in the organizational structure or style of music but in the character qualities of its people—qualities like humility, integrity, brokenness, holiness, love, authenticity, and patience. So embrace the diversity of the body of Christ. Celebrate how Jesus is building His church today in so many different kinds of models and forms. The bride of Christ — the church — is bigger and broader than most people think.

Several years ago, I arrived in Havana from Mexico City. My Cuban friends who were escorting me into Cuba got detained in Mexico City and never even made it to Cuba. So I arrived at the Havana airport without them — and a little confused about what I should do. I knew I was to travel to another city on the island and had to board a train and ride it through the night, but I had no idea who to look for or who was going to meet me.

Arriving early in the morning at the train station, I walked around for about an hour hoping to find someone to help me. Then two old ladies who could not walk very well came in, pointed to me, and said my name. We walked outside, and they gestured for me to hop into the back of a horse-drawn wagon. So I did.

As we began going down the brick roads, I said to myself, *Here I am, being led by these two old grandmothers, and I have no idea who they are or where I am going!* I saw people slowly moving about in the early morning, sweeping their front porches and getting ready for the day. Finally we arrived at a home where a pastor greeted us. I had completely forgotten that it was Sunday. The pastor asked me to preach in his church service, which would begin in two hours. Grateful for the opportunity, I agreed.

The building was only half-finished. Some people sat on the ground, others squatted, and many stood outside. The sound system did not work. Despite these things, the church was filled with life and an authentic expression that would draw anyone interested in the claims of Jesus. There was laughter and joy and a true spirit of brokenness at the same time. It was an amazing time of being with a church.

If you ever have the privilege of visiting churches in oppressed regions of the world, you often will find several common themes among them. One major theme is that the church does not exist solely for itself but is committed to worshiping God and being the body of Christ to the community, no matter what the cost. They live simple lives that are not bound to materialism. They integrate both evangelism and social action and don't think of those as separate ministries. They offer help when someone is in need, such as paying a neighbor's electric bill or providing care for each other's children. They are concerned about other nations knowing about Jesus Christ. They seem to meet together all the time to pray. They love to sing to God and give thanks for who He is and all that He has done. They don't really care what time they get out of church and hardly glance at their watches during the sermon. They give more than 25 to 35 percent of their income away to the church and the poor. They care for the orphans and widows in their own communities.

Surely this is the only model for the church that Jesus would have us all follow!

So I say let the church be the church—in all its multiple expressions and forms—and let it be transformed into the image of Christ and empowered by the Holy Spirit to move out into a world to demonstrate and proclaim the hope that is ours.

FOR REFLECTION AND DISCUSSION

1. In what ways have you been led to believe that we as westerners will be the only ones to win the world to Christ? Do you agree with this?
2. What can you do to help educate yourself on the growth of the body of Christ throughout the world?
3. What does partnership in ministry—whether locally or globally—mean to you?
4. Why do we need each other as the body of Christ throughout the world?
5. Can you think of a time when you experienced the church not reflecting Christ's love? How did you deal with it?

chapter two

THE MEDIUM IMPACTS THE MESSAGE

Not all who wander are lost.
J. R. R. TOLKIEN

F ear. It is something we all experience and live with on different levels. The fears of growing up, being alone, getting married, having no money, going to college, growing old, and dying are common to us all.

Do you know what is the first emotion recorded in the Bible? It is fear. Adam was fearful and hid from God. In Genesis 3:10, Adam says to God, "I was afraid because I was naked; so I hid." Why do you suppose fear is the first recorded emotion in the Bible? Could it be that God is trying to tell us something about the condition of humanity?

I believe that fear is what keeps us from being who God wants us to be and doing what God wants us to do. Some fear is good, as it alerts us of danger. I want my son to experience fear when he approaches a busy street. Yet unhealthy fear is like a ball and chain clamped to our ankle. It keeps us from progressing. Fear of what others may think of us may keep us from loving them. Fear keeps us from pursuing God with our whole hearts because of the change that such a commitment will likely entail.

Beyond all this, fear keeps us, the people of God, from becoming *together* what we can never be *alone.* Often people outside the church see Christians not as a loving, unified family but as a squabbling, malicious mob. Perhaps it is fear that keeps us, as the body of Christ, from loving those who are different from us within the Christian family. It is easy to be around only those who look like us, share our political views, and come from the same economic background. But is that the sort of church that God desires?

Jesus responded in a profound way to the fear of the disciples (see John 20). After He was crucified on the cross, the disciples locked themselves in a room for fear of the Jews. They had given their lives to Jesus but now thought that their teacher and master had abandoned them. And they presumed they were next to be killed. Then Jesus appeared in their midst and said, "Peace be with you!" (verse 19). I am sure that the disciples, upon seeing Jesus, were set free from their fear. Jesus then revealed Himself to them to remove all doubt and said a second time, "Peace be with you! As the Father has sent me, I am sending you" (verse 21). The words of Jesus speak of sending the disciples on missions. The word *missions* does not appear in the Bible, but surely this Scripture is what "missions" is all about. The Father sends the Son. The Son sends the Spirit. The triune God sends all of us who walk with Jesus into a lost and dark world to make disciples of all nations.

Jesus wants to respond to our fear today as He did to the fear of His disciples. Surely Jesus wants to be present in the midst of our fear; He wants to speak to us and reveal Himself to us. He said, "My sheep hear my voice, and I know them, and they follow me" (John 10:27, KJV).

As a teenager I began hearing the voice of Jesus telling me to go and share God's love with peoples and nations that did not live in the luxury that surrounded me in suburban America. School was out, and I was looking forward to summer just like every sixteen-year-old. I had just finished my sophomore year in high school and felt free — no homework or classes for three months. Sleeping in, going out with friends late at night, having parties, going to summer camp — that's what high school kids live for, right? Not me. I wanted something more. I was pursuing

God with my whole heart and wanted to talk to everyone about Him.

During that formative time of my life, something mystical and transcendent happened to me that made me want to be 100 percent sold-out for God. I don't remember it being one event or one specific prayer I prayed. Rather, it was God working to draw me to Himself through everything I experienced or thought.

Following Jesus was all I could think about at that age. Jesus Christ was not just a historical figure or an image that I saw on jewelry. To me He was alive, active, and pursuing my heart, and I wanted to tell everyone. So I told everyone!

A tragic experience involving my high school friend Brian really impacted me. Our brief relationship began in me a deep compassion for those who do not know God. During a ski trip in Colorado, Brian confessed to our group that he did not know God and would end up in hell if he died. I remember feeling overwhelmed that someone would have such a thought. Later Brian and I got together to talk. Sadly, he denied the claims of Christ and did not want to receive Jesus as his Lord. After we returned home, Brian held a shotgun to his face and ended his life. I don't know if Brian ever came to Christ before his suicide; only God knows that. But the thought that there were millions of people in the world who looked at life and death with no hope was more than I could handle—and a cause I wanted to give my life to. I wept for days and could not hold in the pain I felt in my heart for people who did not know God and suffered on a daily basis.

Perhaps other people had been praying for me to develop a heart and love for God and for people, and God heard their prayers. I don't know. But whatever circumstances led to the opportunity for me to go overseas for the first time, it was God who designed it.

My home church organized a small team for a trip to Malawi, Africa. I remember that as I told my friends where I was going, they gave me baffled looks and asked, "Why would you want to go there?" I didn't care what others thought or said. I remember reading the passage in which Jesus says to His disciples, "As the Father has sent me, I am sending you" (John 20:21). I also read, "How, then, can they call on the one they have not believed in? And how can they believe in the one of whom they have not heard? And how can they hear without someone preaching to them? And how can they preach unless they are sent?" (Romans 10:14-15). Through God's Spirit and His Word, I was filled with boldness and did not care what my peers thought.

As I stepped out of the airport in Malawi, my first thought was, *I want to move here and live.* I was like a kid going to the amusement park for the first time and discovering rides I never had imagined. The smells, sounds, and sights were all new to me. Little did I know how this first reaction would change how I was to live my life. I was overcome. I saw a boy chewing what appeared to be a stick. I made the comment too soon, "The people are so hungry here that they are eating sticks." The missionary quickly corrected me and told me that he was eating sugar cane. I immediately said, "I want some of that."

In the days that followed, we worked with a few local churches and schools. Then one day I was asked to preach at a local church. "What will I say?" I asked. "I am only sixteen, and I will be speaking through an interpreter."

I agreed to preach, but I still had doubts. *I will be speaking to so many people older than me,* I thought. *Can I do this?*

I remembered a verse that I had shared with my youth group a few months before at the weekly youth gathering at our church. They were words that Paul wrote to Timothy: "Don't let anyone look down on you because you are young, but set an example for the believers in speech, in life, in love, in faith and in purity. Until I come, devote yourself to the public reading of Scripture, to preaching and to teaching" (1 Timothy 4:12-13).

This empowered me and gave me the confidence I needed. *I can do this!* I thought. Mine wasn't like sermons I had watched others deliver. As I mentioned in the last chapter, I got to offer my first one under a tree, and I was the only white person for miles around. Shirtless mothers nursing their babies, chickens and goats roaming around, and children coming up to me in the middle of the service were all new experiences for me that day. It was actually helpful to speak through an interpreter because I could pause and think about what I was going to say next. I remember preaching on Matthew 7:13-14, the narrow road and the wide road. When I asked if the people sitting there wanted to walk on the narrow road and follow Jesus, several people committed their lives to Christ.

After the service, I was invited to eat lunch at a house that I quickly realized was unlike others in the area. This one actually had walls—it was not a mud hut. As lunch was served, I looked around to discover I was the only white person present—in fact, the only white person present in the entire village. (My team members had received invitations from churches in other areas.) What's more, all of the people from the village were outside watching and singing in my honor. An African pastor, Bombo Chisi, was my host. Though I did not understand it at the time, that experience and my time with this young, dynamic pastor would plant seeds in my heart and give me a love for the indigenous church around the world.

During the lunch, I began to notice something unusual going on and asked my interpreter what was happening. He told me that we were eating at the home of the village chief, who was going to come and join us. I was confused and wondered why he was not already there, but I did not say anything.

I was having fun eating with my hands, as the locals did, and enjoying the new and different tastes. All of a sudden, the chief arrived as loud cheers sounded from outside. I thought, *Wow! This guy must be a pretty important man around here.* He and I greeted each other with the traditional African handshake, and he sat down and began to eat. He soon asked me through the interpreter, "Why are you here?"

I told him that I had come to see his beautiful country and the people who lived there and to tell people about Jesus Christ.

The mood changed, and the chief got very quiet. He and the interpreter began to talk, and their calm exchange seemed to escalate into an argument. In the midst of their conversation, the chief slammed down his fist a few times in obvious anger.

I asked what was going on, and the interpreter said the chief did not want me to talk about Jesus Christ anymore. I didn't know what to think. But, sensing the Holy Spirit's urging, I told the interpreter that I would like to humbly share a few thoughts with the chief before I left. I began to tell him what the gospel meant to me as I understood it at that age, and I told him that this was not just an opinion of a youngster from America as he might think.

As the conversation continued, he slammed his fist down on the table and began yelling at the interpreter; then he walked out of his own home. I could not believe it. Had I insulted an important man in his own home? Suddenly I grew very afraid and began to wonder if I would make it out of there alive. Some time later, the chief came back in and talked to the pastor, who was his friend. We finished lunch, and I played with the chief's children. The chief was cordial to me as I left. Before long, some local missionaries arrived in their van to pick me up. As you might imagine, I was glad to see them.

But that's not the end of the story. A few weeks after I arrived home, I received a letter from my interpreter. He told me that the chief I'd met was not just the leader of that particular village; he was ruler of more than a hundred villages in that region. He was not just an *important* man but a *powerful* man as well. And he was a well-known leader. The interpreter also told me that the chief was hostile toward Christianity in his country and strove to stop its growth by mistreating Christians and making them pay more taxes.

The interpreter wrote that for years he and other Christian leaders had tried to share Christ with this chief and had enlisted many people to pray for him. At the end of the letter, he told me that after we left

Malawi, the chief had decided to follow Christ and change his ways.

I was so thrilled. In closing the letter, the interpreter said the chief remembered the day I spoke about Christ at such a young age. I was not afraid to speak to such an important man so clearly and with confidence. The pastor from Malawi said that he believed the Holy Spirit used that time to convict the chief in his process of coming to Christ.

As I reflect on that encounter, a verse in the Bible comes to mind: "God hath chosen the foolish things of the world to confound the wise" (1 Corinthians 1:27, KJV). I had been foolish, in a sense, for failing to properly understand the situation over lunch. But it is not important what I did or said. What matters is what God did through me as I made myself available. God wants not our *ability* but our *availability*, regardless of our age, education, vocation, ethnicity, or possessions. God wants us to give our fears to Him and simply be available to be used.

THE MYSTERY OF SALVATION

The greatest gift we have in the world is the free gift of salvation through Christ. I have shared this truth with people all around the world. I have told many people from other religions that God has initiated relationship with us. The difference between Christianity and other faiths is that all other religions are based on people's efforts and works to lead them to God, Karma, or enlightenment. But the great news of the gospel is God making the first move by sending Jesus Christ to earth. God demonstrates His love for us *first*, to show us that we do not have to do anything to deserve or earn God's love for us.

The basic premise of coming to Christ is something so glorious and beautiful that, in reality, it is sometimes difficult to put into words. But it is not a complicated concept. Jesus said we must become like a little child to enter the kingdom of heaven (see Matthew 18:3). Indeed, faith in God comes easily for children.

Salvation that allows us to know God and have a home in heaven includes these qualities:

It is a mystery and a work of the Holy Spirit. Salvation is foundationally a work of the Holy Spirit. People often ask me, "How do you convert people?" I answer, "I don't—the Holy Spirit does."

God's Spirit convicts and converts people, not our words or actions. In John 3, Jesus talks to a religious man who asks him how to have eternal life.

> *"I tell you the truth, no one can enter the kingdom of God unless he is born of water and the Spirit. Flesh gives birth to flesh, but the Spirit gives birth to spirit. You should not be surprised at my saying, 'You must be born again.' The wind blows wherever it pleases. You hear its sound, but you cannot tell where it comes from or where it is going. So it is with everyone born of the Spirit." (verses 5-8)*

The Greek word for "Spirit" in this passage is *pneuma*. This word can be translated as "wind"—as in, "You don't know where the wind is blowing; so it is with the spirit of God, who allows this new birth to take place in people's hearts."

It is not by our own efforts or works. As the apostle Paul explained, "it is by grace you have been saved, through faith—and this not from yourselves, it is the gift of God—not by works, so that no one can boast" (Ephesians 2:8-9). Salvation is free. We cannot buy it, earn it, or work for it. We cannot be a good enough person, go to spiritual meetings enough, meditate enough, or perform religious duties enough to receive salvation. It is a gift from God.

It is solely by the goodness, grace, and love of God. Paul wrote, "God demonstrates his own love for us in this: While we were still sinners, Christ died for us" (Romans 5:8). It is only by the grace and goodness of God that we can receive salvation. God saves us; we don't save ourselves. His love for us is too great to comprehend or imagine.

There is no love as pure and real as God's, and He demonstrated it purely in Jesus Christ.

Jesus Christ is the sole means of salvation. When you closely study the teachings of Jesus, you will notice the exclusivity of His claims. He was not an inclusive teacher when it came to the means of salvation. That is, Jesus declared unequivocally that believing in Him is the *only* way to be saved. He said, "I am the way and the truth and the life. No one comes to the Father except through me" (John 14:6). Elsewhere, He proclaimed, "Enter through the narrow gate. For wide is the gate and broad is the road that leads to destruction, and many enter through it. But small is the gate and narrow the road that leads to life, and only a few find it" (Matthew 7:13-14). A relationship with God can be achieved only through Jesus Christ.

It is something we participate in throughout life. Some people have the misconception that salvation only involves saying a prayer and leaving it at that. But salvation is meant to be "worked out" through our whole lives — not to be earned, but to be deepened and nurtured in the grace and knowledge of Jesus Christ. Paul emphasized this point: "My dear friends, as you have always obeyed — not only in my presence, but now much more in my absence — continue to work out your salvation with fear and trembling, for it is God who works in you to will and to act according to his good purpose" (Philippians 2:12-13). This process, called sanctification, means that we are to become set apart and made holy, as Christ was holy. This will take our whole lives, and we will never reach perfection until we get to heaven.

WHEN THE GOOD NEWS IS COMMUNICATED BADLY

The church's message is many times not the message of Jesus at all. Some churches insist that a certain political ideology must be embraced in order for you to be included in the kingdom of God. Some in the church even advocate "making Jesus your choice so you can drive a

Rolls Royce." But did following Jesus entail economic gain for the first-century disciples? Hardly. Sometimes the church speaks of certain cultural standards and rules that must be followed: "Don't do this . . . listen to that . . . dress like this . . . don't wear your hair like that," and *then* you can have a relationship with Jesus. Such arbitrary requirements and unbiblical promises certainly do not reflect the true gospel of Christ.

But even when the message of the gospel is right on, often the way we share it is way off. In other words, when we communicate ineffectively, the real substance and significance of the gospel get lost in translation. Why is this?

- *The medium distorts the message.* Sometimes the way the church proclaims the good news of salvation is like broadcasting the most beautiful symphony through a cheap transistor radio. So often *how* we communicate the gospel does not do justice to the message itself.

  If you travel much, you know that you can hear the English language spoken in many different ways — from rural Mississippi to the Bronx to the Pacific Northwest to England to Australia to someone speaking English as a second language. When you hear people speak English with a different accent or cadence, it can be difficult to focus on the meaning of the words because you're distracted by the manner in which they're spoken.

  Similarly, many people have misconceptions about Jesus because His "representatives" distort the gospel by communicating ineffectively. When some people think of Christianity, they picture a guy yelling on the street corner, a lady on TV with big hair and bigger jewelry, or a million other images. Christians who speak the truth without love or love without truth send an incomplete, and perhaps even incorrect, message about Christ and His teaching.

- *It appears that we're selling a product.* So often the way we've been told to share our faith comes across as a sales presentation. The goal is to "close the deal" and then move on to the next customer. I actually had a person who sincerely loves God ask me, "How do you close the deal?" I was taken aback. Sharing the gospel is not about getting people to "sign on the dotted line"; it's about helping people understand the amazing gift of God's love. We don't do anyone (least of all God) any favors by thinking that evangelism involves quotas, a slick sales pitch, and tactics for selling a commodity.

  Our attitude should always be saturated in humility, grace, and compassion. Augustine had a prayer that I believe speaks to understanding how we should share our faith. "Lord, allow me to be with those who are seeking the truth, but deliver me from those who think they have found it." None of us knows everything. We are not completely "there." We are not completely sanctified or holy, nor do we think and behave in godly ways 24/7. We strive for that but realize that we are not there and therefore do not pretend to be.

Here are a few thoughts about presenting the good news both humbly and effectively:

Share your faith while admitting you have much to learn on this journey called life. St. Francis of Assisi wrote, "Seek to understand rather than to be understood." Sharing your faith is not about controlling the conversation and telling someone what you know. Being honest and open about your own struggles and fears is much more powerful than telling the other person how he or she needs to change. Some in the church identify those who come to faith as no longer being seekers. Instead, they identify only pre–Christ-followers as "seekers." This implies that after we have accepted Christ, we are no longer seeking. Can't we still be seekers after coming to Christ? I believe we can be and should be. But in sharing our faith, we often do not come to people with this attitude.

Share your faith in community. Faith journeys are not meant to be lived alone. Lesslie Newbigin, the famous missionary to India, has aptly described Christian community as the interpretation of the gospel. Authentic Christian community embodies both the gospel's message and its essence. We convey the gospel to the world not only through what we say but also through the vibrant life we share together in community.[1]

We need redemption, and we need a community of people to share it with. Inviting friends and family who are not followers of Jesus to be a part of your Christian community is very fruitful. People should see how followers of Christ spend their money, relate to their spouses, encourage each other, and share their possessions with each other in times of need. Some Christians harbor a "separatist" attitude that holds them back from building genuine community with people of non-faith. But this attitude is based in fear and has nothing to do with the apostle John's admonition to keep ourselves from the entice-ments of this world (see 1 John 2:15).

Share faith in service to your community and the world. You can allow lost people to engage with issues of the gospel by inviting them to join your church in serving the poor in your community or other areas. Mission work, locally and globally, is not solely for "mature Christians"; it can provide an open door for the skeptic to choose to follow or return to Jesus. I have heard many people tell stories of how building a house for a poor family or serving orphans was a key step in coming to Christ for the first time or returning to the faith after being away. Before my wife and I were married, she led missions teams to Honduras to plant trees after Hurricane Mitch severely damaged the ecosystem. Through these teams, both participants and locals who volunteered came to faith in Jesus Christ. It is through serving that you — and others — are transformed.

Share how Christ has changed you. The greatest thing you can share is your life. People don't want to be preached at; they want a friend. They want to hear stories, and the greatest story you can tell is your own. They want to hear how Christ has come alive in your heart and become a friend to you.

Realize that it is the working of the Holy Spirit—not what you say or don't say—that points people to Jesus. The work of the Holy Spirit is a mystery. Jesus said, "The wind blows wherever it pleases. You hear its sound, but you cannot tell where it comes from or where it is going. So it is with everyone born of the Spirit" (John 3:8). We must remain dependent on the Spirit while sharing our faith and always rely on this truth: Engaging people's hearts in spiritual matters and bringing them to Christ is the *Holy Spirit's* work, not ours.

One year while ministering in India, we were up in a small village near Darjeeling (where the tea is grown), and I was to speak to a church that met in a small home in the Himalayan Mountains. At the last moment, my friend from India was called away to speak at another church—and he was my interpreter! So there I was with no interpreter, and I was supposed to preach in one hour.

A woman approached me and asked if I needed an interpreter. Of course, I immediately said, "Yes! Please, will you interpret for me?"

She agreed, and we began to get to know each other. The first thing she told me was that she did not believe in Jesus Christ. At first I thought, *She can't possibly interpret for me*. But then I began to sense that God had sent her and allowed our paths to cross. I asked her to please translate what I said word for word. We prayed before the service—actually, I prayed. And we were off.

After the three-hour service, my interpreter came up to me and said she wanted to talk. She began telling me she had been considering the claims of Christ for a few months but did not really understand because she had no access to a Bible. So for the first time, she actually heard the claims of Christ by interpreting my message.

After hearing my simple sermon that morning, she decided to follow Christ as the one true God and not the millions of Hindu gods. I was overjoyed! What a strange—and divine—confluence of circumstances.

You never know where people have been prior to the moment they hear the gospel. You never know how the Spirit of God has been working, convicting, and moving in their hearts. We cannot predict when or how those around us might put their faith in Christ. All we can do is remain humble, keep seeking, and be faithful in sharing the hope we have as followers of Jesus. As Philemon 6 says, "Be active in sharing your faith, so you will have a full understanding of every good thing we have in Christ."

FOR REFLECTION AND DISCUSSION

1. Take a few moments to think about how you came to Christ. (If you're in a group setting, briefly tell your story.) What was the most important factor that led you to Christ? Can you detect similar themes from other Christians?

2. Think of a time when you heard someone share Christ in a positive and healthy way. What specifically gave you this impression?

3. Have you heard someone share Christ in a way you considered damaging or counterproductive? What specifically gave you this impression?

4. When it comes to faith sharing, why is loving people from the heart more important than "knowing the right information"?

chapter three

JESUS, THE SINGER FROM AMERICA?

"I have other sheep that are not of this sheep pen. I must bring them also. They too will listen to my voice, and there shall be one flock and one shepherd."

JESUS CHRIST

The purpose of theology is to change the world for the better.

DIETRICH BONHOEFFER

One year while in India, several missions partners and I embarked on a long train ride. We were off to visit a new outreach site where there were no churches in existence. It was virgin territory as far as the gospel was concerned.

You have never had a real train experience until you've ridden a train in India. People bring their chickens, goats, and other animals on the train with them. The smells and noises you hear are unlike anything you have encountered in your life. At night, you had better chain your suitcase to your seat or it will surely be gone by morning. Even going to the bathroom is an amazing experience. The bathroom is essentially a small compartment with a hole in the floor that opens to the train tracks below. That's right, when you "gotta go," it just goes right out onto the tracks!

The ride we thought would take twenty hours ended up taking more than forty. During those seemingly endless hours, I explored the train, counted goats, and spent lots of time staring out at the beautiful Indian terrain. At one point, I began to play my guitar, and my friends and I sang together. All the other passengers on our train cart gathered close to hear the young Americans sing. After a while, I noticed one man in particular. I asked him through an interpreter, "Do you know who we are singing about?"

The man said he didn't.

I then told him we had just sung a song about Jesus Christ.

"Who is He?" the man replied. "A singer from America?"

I couldn't believe it. When I tell that story in churches and at conferences, I am repeatedly surprised by the laughter that comes from the crowd. I often ponder why the crowd is laughing. Some crowds laugh louder than others, and I believe that the ones who laugh least recognize the power in that story and the heaviness it brings to my heart. How could that man not know who Jesus Christ is? Why would his only connection to the name of Jesus be through a happenstance encounter with a group of Americans on a train?

While I was a college student, I was elated with the opportunity to return to Malawi. To be able to return to a distant part of the world and visit old friends from another culture was a blessing. The idea of traveling to another part of the world and *never* developing long-term relationships seemed so futile to me. Perhaps I could meet the chief of that region again or find the elephant that ate my camera.

Upon my arrival, an African pastor informed me that the next day we were going to visit the chief whom I had shared the gospel with on my previous visit. At our meeting the following day, the chief and I visited together for several minutes, and then he invited me to his house for a meal after the church service. I got to speak to the same church that once met under a tree and that I had preached my first sermon to at the age of sixteen. The church now had a brick building, and many members expressed thanks to me for returning to their village. The pastor asked people to raise their hands if they remembered me from four years earlier. So many raised their hands that I could not believe it!

When the church service was over, several of us walked for twenty minutes through the tall grass to the chief's house. I told my traveling companions that when we arrived, we should eat with our hands because that is the custom in African villages. I wanted my friends to know I was an "expert" in cross-cultural affairs. I was sure they would all be so impressed. We sat down and began to eat with our hands but soon looked around to discover all the children eating with spoons! They were staring at us, no doubt wondering why these *goozungus* (white men) were displaying such poor manners. Needless to say, I was the laughingstock of the trip.

We were in the middle of nowhere, and there was no electricity. It seemed we were a hundred miles past the Great Commission. I remember thinking, *I could not be farther from civilization than I am right now.* But then the most amazing thing happened. Our hosts brought each of us a bottle of Coke. I was shocked even further to realize that it was cold—ice cold! I thought, *How could I be in the middle of a village in southeast Africa and be drinking a cold American beverage?*

It turns out that Coca-Cola products are available just about anywhere you go. Whether you are in the deserts of the Middle East, the jungles of Africa, or the villages of India, Coke is right there with you. If you go to the Coca-Cola museum in Atlanta, Georgia, you will be amazed at the way the brand has managed to infiltrate the entire globe. Their product is known and recognized by almost everyone on our planet. Why, then, I wonder, has it been two thousand years since Jesus Christ came, yet the gospel has still never been heard in many parts of the world? Someone once asked why so much time, money, and energy is spent in trying to *recommunicate* the gospel message to those who have heard it over and over again, when a billion people on our planet have never heard it once.

A pastor in Pakistan once told me that every demon has to memorize one verse. It is Matthew 24:14: "The gospel of the Kingdom must be preached to every nation and then the end shall come" (PAR). The pastor said that this verse is written on every demon's bed. They have to read it every night. And before they come to the earth to tempt and try to destroy Christians, they have to recite the verse to Satan himself.

The Devil and his demons know that if the gospel goes to every nation, then the end will come. When the gospel is preached, the orphan and widow are cared for, the oppressed are empowered, and the church's power is unleashed. When that happens, the chambers of hell shudder in fear. The demonic forces recoil when the people of God are fueled with passion for His glory in all the earth, and they dread the day when the gospel is shared with all people.

I am not suggesting we focus our energy on knowing exactly when Christ will return—after all, the Bible makes clear that pinpointing His coming is impossible. Many Christians are fascinated by eschatology, the study of the end times. Just look at the LEFT BEHIND fiction series and its popularity among Christians. I believe it's possible for such a focus to produce passivity and laziness in regard to spreading the gospel throughout the world. "Why do anything?" one may ask. "Jesus is coming anyway!"

When our attention is captured by looking for "signs of the end," we run the risk of not seeing and responding to the poor, lost, and dying around us in the world right now. When someone asks me what my theology of eschatology is, I always say, "I only have a missiological eschatology." What I mean is that everything in our Christian theology should be missional. Our study and worship of God should always connect with the ministry of the church to the world. I do think we should long for the coming of Jesus because the Bible says there will be a crown in heaven for those who do (see 2 Timothy 4:8). But we should not spend all of our time and energy discussing and debating about it. There is simply too much work to do.

It is reported that Martin Luther was once asked what he would do if he knew Jesus were to return the next day. He responded, "I would plant a tree!"[1] It seems to me that Luther was saying there's work to be done with a future hope and beauty in mind. He had a long-term perspective, and so should we.

A HEART FOR THE LOST

Many of Jesus' teachings focus on His heart for those who are not in relationship with the Father. Indeed this is a central theme in many of His parables. But perhaps the clearest proclamation He ever made regarding the motivation of His heart is recorded in Luke 19:10: "For the Son of Man came to seek and to save what was lost."

Have you ever traveled somewhere in the world and been completely lost? I have many times. I've been lost in countries where I could not find one person who spoke English or one sign I could read. It has happened to me in places like Baghdad, Iraq, and Dhaka, Bangladesh, and countless villages throughout India. It is an utterly helpless feeling to be totally lost. In a similar way, everyone in the world is born helpless and in need of Jesus Christ. This is our reality, plain and simple.

Jesus never stops calling people to Him. He said, "I am the good shepherd; I know my sheep and my sheep know me—just as the Father knows me and I know the Father—and I lay down my life for the sheep. I have other sheep that are not of this sheep pen. I must bring them also" (John 10:14-16). Sometimes the people Jesus calls are the very ones we have given up on.

The outcasts of society are often ignored by the church, no matter which culture you look at in the world. This group includes orphans, drug abusers, victims of violence, the poor, people with HIV and AIDS, migrant workers, adults and children trafficked into sexual and other forms of slavery, the illiterate, the displaced, and those who are deprived of national identity. These are the kinds of people who, in my opinion, Jesus would identify with if He were here in the flesh today.

After all, it was Jesus who said,

> *"When you give a luncheon or dinner, do not invite your friends, your brothers or relatives, or your rich neighbors; if you do, they may invite you back and so you will be repaid. But when you give a banquet, invite the poor, the crippled, the lame, the blind, and you will be blessed. Although they cannot repay you, you will be repaid at the resurrection of the righteous." (Luke 14:12-14)*

Within Christian circles, you will often hear people inquire about how big a particular church is—meaning how many members it has. "How many people attend that church?" they ask. I believe Jesus is not merely counting those who are in the church; He is counting those who are not. I always try to remember this as I travel through the world and ask that God will continue to break my heart for the lost, the hurting, and the destitute. Remember the words of Jesus to His disciples: "Do you not say, 'Four months more and then the harvest'? I tell you, open your eyes and look at the fields! They are ripe for harvest" (John 4:35).

SO MANY HAVE NOT HEARD

In the world today, over one billion live in regions where they cannot hear about Jesus Christ, whether through a local church or a friend. Why can't they hear about Christ? Because there are no Christians there to tell them. Yes, God is able to reveal Himself through miraculous means, as he did to Saul on the road to Damascus, but most often God uses people to convey His love and grace to others.

If you travel to a small town like Brownwood, Texas, you will most likely not meet a Buddhist. Do you think the people in that community regularly hear about Buddhism? Perhaps they might see Richard Gere on television talking about his Buddhist beliefs, or they might read a story in the paper about the Dalai Lama's advocacy for his own Tibetan people. But in all probability, few individuals in that community will ever engage in spiritual discussions regarding the teachings of Buddhism. A similar reality exists for thousands of villages, towns, and cities around the world where church communities are not present. This is not mere speculation—I have witnessed this firsthand. In northern countries of Africa, throughout the Middle East, across India and China, and in other pockets in Asia, the church is conspicuously absent. People cannot explore and understand the Christian faith, simply because there are no Christians available to explain it. Even in a city of 300,000, there may be only a handful of families who name Jesus Christ as Lord.

How will people who do not know Christ come to know Him if there are no Christians around? The answer: It will be very difficult. We must let this stark reality awaken within us a compassion that compels us to action. As Paul wrote,

How, then, can they call on the one they have not believed in? And how can they believe in the one of whom they have not heard? And how can they hear without someone preaching to them? And how can they preach unless they are sent? As it is written, "How beautiful are the feet of those who bring good news!" (Romans 10:14-15)

We live in communities in America where it seems there is a church on every corner. Too often we define "pioneer" ministry as simply retelling the gospel in ways that are relatable and relevant to those in America who already have some understanding of Christ (though it may be inaccurate) and who have had some experience of church (though it may not have been relevant or meaningful). While this is healthy and needed, we must not neglect those regions of the world where the church of Jesus Christ is still sparse or even nonexistent. We must encourage the church to always think globally about God's redemptive plan for the world.

Several years ago, I spent the entire summer in East Indonesia in a place called Irian Jaya. Only a few decades ago, the people of this region were cannibals and had little or no contact with outside cultures. All summer long, my teammates and I worked to construct a wall around a training center for pastors. We lived with the students and shared meals with them. I will never forget when our team said farewell to the new friends we had met during our time there. They literally wept for hours on our shoulders because we were leaving. I will forever be moved by the sorrow they expressed over the likelihood that we would not see each other again until we got to heaven.

There is a need for us as followers of Jesus to be filled with grief and sorrow over the millions of people on our planet who are separated from God. Luke tells us that "as [Jesus] approached Jerusalem and saw the city, he wept over it" (19:41). The meaning of the word *wept* here is not a silent cry. The Greek word is *klaio*, which means to sob and wail. I like what Bible commentator Matthew Henry says about this moment in Jesus' life: "The great Ambassador from heaven is here making his public entry into Jerusalem, not to be respected there, but to be rejected; he knew what a nest of vipers he was throwing himself into."[2] He knew he went to die at the hands of the world, yet he wept *for them*.

Jesus cares deeply for the lost, even though He knows many of them will reject Him. His tenacious love for the world reverberates through His teachings. He said He would leave the ninety-nine sheep for the one that was lost and will rejoice when a single lost coin is found (see Luke 15:3-10).

THE SACRIFICE HAS BEEN MADE

Going to Varanasi, India, for the first time was an overwhelming experience for me. Varanasi is the Mecca of Hinduism—meaning that it is the holiest city in the Hindu religion. There are more than twenty-five thousand Hindu temples there, and the holy river, the Ganges, runs through the city. Hindus believe that if you bathe in this holy river, your sins will be removed and you will break the cycle of reincarnation. They also believe that the cycle of reincarnation can be broken if your body is cremated in Varanasi after you die. It is a holy city, yet it's filled with much hopelessness.

One day in this city, I was sitting with an Indian pastor and we were praying for these people. After some time in prayer, the pastor told me a story that will haunt me for as long as I live. A girl, probably eighteen years old, came to the Ganges River in Varanasi with her only child. She walked to the Ganges weighed down with guilt and shame over her sins. She believed she had to sacrifice her only child to the gods in order to be forgiven. Lifting the baby in the air, she said some mantras (Hindu prayers) and then threw the child into the river. A local Indian evangelist was watching from a distance and could not believe what he was seeing. *This woman must be on drugs, or maybe she's gone mad*, he thought. He ran down to her and asked, "What is wrong? What have you done?"

The poor Hindu girl replied, "The sins on my heart are too many, so I had to offer the best I have to the gods in order for my sins to be removed. I offered my own child."

"You did not have to do that!" exclaimed the evangelist. "Your sins have been paid for in the death of Jesus Christ. His blood has been shed, and we can receive the forgiveness of all our sin. Our hearts can be washed white as snow."

The girl looked despondent. "Why could you not have come just five minutes before to tell me this amazing news? Then I would not have had to throw my own child into the river."

IF YOU'RE GOING TO BE A LIGHT, BE A BIG LIGHT

When I was a kid in Sunday school, I used to sing this song: "This little light of mine, I'm gonna let it shine, let it shine, let it shine, let it shine." Sound familiar?

Even as a child singing this ditty, I always thought, *I don't want to be a little light—I want to be a* big *light*. I didn't like the implication that I could do only little things for God. I wanted to do big things for Him.

How about you? Since Christians are the light of the world, what do you say we burn as brightly as possible?

If you ever travel by plane to Las Vegas at night, you will no doubt see a bright beam of light shining into the sky. It comes from the Luxor Hotel and Casino. It is the brightest light in the world (or so it is promoted). The average lightbulb used to illuminate a room is sixty or seventy-five watts. The average bulb at the Luxor is 350,000 watts. It is said that if you were sitting in a spacecraft ten miles above the earth, you could read a newspaper by the light of the Luxor. In an airplane flying at thirty thousand feet, you can see the Luxor light from 250 miles away.

Jesus said,

"You are the light of the world. A city on a hill cannot be hidden. Neither do people light a lamp and put it under a bowl. Instead they put it on its stand, and it gives light to everyone in the house. In the same way, let your light shine before men, that they may see your good deeds and praise your Father in heaven." (Matthew 5:14-16)

I fully believe that when the lostness of humanity breaks our hearts and consumes us, we will begin to grasp a portion of God's love for the world, and we will never be the same. We will want our lives, our families, and our churches to be lights that shine brightly in the world. We will spend our money differently and take vacations differently. We will consume less so we can give away more. We will do all we can to serve as a beacon pointing the way home, where the Father is watching and waiting.

ENGAGING SOMEONE FROM ANOTHER RELIGION

I believe it is helpful to study other beliefs to know how to engage in a conversation with someone from another religion. But when you talk with someone from another faith, it is important to see past the rituals and doctrines so you can get to more fundamental issues.

Let's take Hinduism, for example. Within Hindu culture, there are dozens of festivals. If you ask ten Hindus about the meaning of a particular festival — say, Divali — you will most likely get ten different answers. Although Divali is perhaps the most important festival, many devout Hindus approach it differently and draw different meanings from it. This is not like our experience as Christians. If you ask a bunch of devout Christians about the true meaning of Easter, you will usually get only one response: Easter is a celebration of the resurrection of Jesus Christ.

I was once in Kathmandu, Nepal, during the Divali festival, which is also known as the Festival of Lights. It looks like Christmastime because every shop and house is covered in glimmering lights, which are said to attract the attention of the gods. The day before I arrived was the Divali "crow *puja*." (*Puja* means "worship.") The day I attended was the "dog puja," and the day after that was the "cow puja." Hindus worship various animals because each represents a different Hindu god.

Dogs, for example, represent Lord Bhairab. I actually kept the front page of the Kathmandu Post from the day I attended the festival. On it there is a photo of a bunch of police dogs in training. Their fur is covered with flowers, and tikas were applied to their foreheads. The article described how the policemen worship the dogs on that day. It was not something you would see on the front page of most major American newspapers.

I say all this to illustrate how the festivals take on different meanings for different Hindus, depending on their role in life and what part of the country they are from. A Hindu living in London is probably going to have a different interpretation from a Hindu living in a small village regarding what the festival of Divali (or any other festival) is supposed to mean.

This leads to an important principle when discussing faith with a Hindu (or, for that matter, a person from any faith system). When I engage Hindus, I *first* try to listen and learn about the meaning of the festival from their point of view, and then I try to draw bridges of similarity between their belief and my own faith in Jesus Christ. For example, I often ask questions such as, "What brings you hope about this certain Hindu god or festival?" Or, "How does this help you love better and become a better person?" Or, "How does this allow you to have peace at night for the wrongs you have done?" All of these questions allow me, in turn, to share how I have found hope, forgiveness, peace, and love in Christ.

By focusing the conversation on our shared values—finding meaning, peace, contentment in life, or the ability to love those who wrong us—I can easily share my own story or a story from the Bible in an inoffensive way. All the while, of course, I am praying that the Holy Spirit will allow this person to see Jesus and desire to learn more about Him.

Usually the Hindus in India and Nepal are happy to talk about these issues, as they typically have never explored their rituals to consider their deeper meaning. In fact, I've found that most people in the

ServLife Workers in Nepal Build Relationships and Share Their Faith

world, regardless of their religion, love to talk about the significant issues of meaning, purpose, and identity that all human beings search for. So when engaging people from other faiths, approach them with an attitude of curiosity, asking a lot of questions rather than offering a lot of answers. If you do this, you will usually get a chance later in the conversation to share your perspective.

RUN TO THE PAIN AND EMBRACE IT – DON'T HIDE!

Without passion for the lost, Christians tend to fall into a defensive posture in life. We start our own schools, develop our own business networks, establish our own health clubs, and totally insulate ourselves from those who do not know God. We do it all in the name of "keeping ourselves pure" or "setting an example," but that is not what happens most of the time. The sad truth is that we create these facilities mostly for our own comfort. I have never had anyone tell me that they came to Jesus because they saw a church build a three-million-dollar health club.

Why does the church in the West fall into the trap of "keeping up with the Joneses"? The most important fruits that can come out of church facilities are relationships and conversations that lead people to know Christ. But doesn't it make more sense to *go to the lost where they are* rather than try to *lure them into our facilities*? Of course, I'm not saying the church should never own land or build its own structures. There is sound financial wisdom in owning property. I just wonder at times how Jesus would respond if He walked the earth today and saw churches filled with shops, espresso bars, and elaborate water fountains costing in the hundreds of thousands of dollars.

Consider what's happened over the past few decades in the urban centers of many North American cities. A lot of churches in those areas have dwindled to very small congregations as most Christians move to the suburbs. Has our desire for the "American dream" kept us from living the life that Jesus has called us to live? For many in the western world, the answer is yes. Why has the church not run to the rough neighborhoods and high-crime areas to be the presence of Christ there and to impact those areas for positive change? Have we prioritized our own safety and growing our church budget at the expense of living a life of mission and going to where the poor and hurting are?

Thankfully, many followers of Jesus are not satisfied with this "retreat mentality" and are moving back to the urban centers. The crime rate may be higher and the schools may not be as good as in the suburbs, but the believers are there to fulfill God's mission. They are putting their kids into public schools and teaching them to be missionaries there.

Many other Christians are going to countries labeled "unsafe" by the U.S. State Department—countries filled with people in need of the love of God. They are not letting anything stop them from finding a way to get there, even if it means selling their possessions.

Am I saying that every Christian should move to an inner-city neighborhood or to a foreign country in order to do God's will? My short answer is no. Not everyone has to move somewhere else to be used powerfully by God. You can bloom right where you've been planted. But if you are not being stretched and challenged in your walk with God, then I encourage you to move someplace where you *will* be stretched and challenged. That could mean across town or across the ocean. You can find a job in any city in the world teaching English or any number of other needed skills. And all urban centers in America have affordable areas to live. It might not be in the area you prefer, but it will be among those you most need to help.

As Christ followers, we cannot live by and be conformed to the systems of the world, which are greed, materialism, lust, pride, and self-centeredness. As the Bible says, "But just as he who called you is holy, so be holy in all you do; for it is written: 'Be holy, because I am holy'" (1 Peter 1:15-16). We need wisdom and counsel on how not to be conformed to this world. At the same time, we cannot constantly point a finger at our culture and say the problem is only with "them." Many Christians expressed grave concern when prayer was taken out of schools, but I think God is more concerned when Christians stop praying. In a similar way, some Christians accused our society of losing moral clarity when the Ten Commandments were removed from public areas. I assert that it is more of a problem when the followers of Jesus stop living and obeying them. As Jesus said, "Don't point out the toothpick in someone else's eye when you have a telephone pole in your own eye" (PAR). The tendency to isolate, point fingers, and judge is something we Christians must be careful to avoid.

Instead, look at the culture around you as the missionary Christ has called you to be, and constantly pray for ways to connect and relate to those in your sphere of influence. Perhaps it will be through music, photography, travel, sports, hiking, or art. Whatever it is, begin to simply see that people are people, no matter how they dress, talk, look, or smell. They are simply people who need to hear, experience, and know about the love of God.

✂ — ✂

We approached a police roadblock at about ten at night after driving for over six hours from Kathmandu, Nepal. Albert and I had missed our flight to ServLife India on the border of India and Nepal for our pastors training conference. I realized our driver would not pass the roadblock no matter much I urged him to drive on. He said we would be shot by the Royal Nepal Army if he drove past the roadblock. There was no one in sight on the road. We were surrounded by mountains in the middle of nowhere. He said he did not want to die that night, and I had to agree — not because I fear death but because I want to have more children, watch my son grow up, grow old with my wife, and see the gospel preached around the world.

We turned around, realizing we were going to have to find a place to stay. At that late hour, it would be very difficult. We passed several houses, which were all locked up. Finally, we saw one small hut with a fire blazing inside. We got out of the car, and a poor Nepali family welcomed us into the hut. We sat around their fire and shared stories. They said that two days earlier, twenty-four soldiers had been killed by Maoists a short way down the road. That was why the roadblocks had been set up. The local police had also discovered two dozen bombs intended for the destruction of supply trucks. Even as the family told us this, I watched a truck park right in front of the hut, making me wonder how many bombs *hadn't* been found and confiscated.

When the mother of this family found out we operated an orphanage and children's home, she brought us a small girl and asked us to take her. She said that her village of four hundred people had more than forty-five orphans, a result of the violent Maoist conflict. We told her that our facility was not equipped to take more children at that time but that I would keep in touch with her.

We prayed for the family and shared the gospel. We also gave the woman some extra medicine for the children in the community. It was Thanksgiving Day when this happened, and I told her about the holiday. Then she showed us to an empty room, where we slept on a wooden floor with one blanket. Worse, I did not have warm clothing. As I lay down to sleep, I was cold and hungry. I had eaten only one meal that day, on our plane ride twelve hours earlier.

I began to ask myself, *Why am I here—and missing my son's second birthday? I am cold and hungry and far from my wife. I could be many places right now with my family, and here I am, stranded in the middle of the mountains, hiding out in a grass hut, surrounded by Maoist rebels.*

I was reminded at that moment that it is the love of God that motivates me. When we woke at five the next morning, the barrier had been removed, and we were able to drive to Raxaul, the home of ServLife India. After getting to the pastors conference, my heart was filled with deep joy at seeing a dream become reality. God wants us to create opportunities to love people when those opportunities align with His redemptive purposes for a lost world. To see a movement of indigenous young Indians giving their lives to preach the gospel and start churches among their own people is what ServLife is all about. There is no greater cause in the world than seeing the love of God extended to every person on the globe.

I encourage you to meditate on the following adaptation of Psalm 23. It is not written as most know it but paraphrased from the perspective of one who does not know God. This is how millions of people in the world think, feel, and live their lives without knowing God through Jesus Christ:

I have no shepherd.
I want and am in need.
I have no one to feed me in green pastures, I have no rest.

I have no one to lead me to quiet waters.
I am thirsty.
I have no one to guide me in the right ways.
I don't know where to turn.
As I walk through the valley of the shadow of death, evil surrounds
*   me;*
I am terribly afraid for no one is with me to comfort me.
I have no feast prepared for me.
I am overwhelmed by my enemies.
No one anoints my wounds or fills my cup.
My cup is empty.
All the days of my life are filled with disappointment and deceit.
I have no home for eternity.
Will I dwell in an evil house forever?[3]

FOR REFLECTION AND DISCUSSION

1. How do you make an intentional effort to reach out to someone who does not know God?
2. What could you do to meet more people who do not know God or are curious about the things of God?
3. Who do you know that is from another religion? How might you effectively engage with this person to discuss his or her faith?
4. What are some ways you have isolated yourself from the lost world around you? How could you begin to reengage the world in a healthy way?
5. How can you practically help lost people in other cultures around the world come to know God?

chapter four

MONEY: ENABLER OR ENTANGLER?

The love of worldly possessions is a sort of birdlime,
which entangles the soul and prevents it flying to God.

AUGUSTINE OF HIPPO

Riches are the instrument of all vices, because they
render us capable of putting even our worst desires
into execution.

AMBROSE

Several years ago, I returned to the Sudanese refugee camps in Uganda. I planned to meet with a number of pastors to determine ways our organization could serve and support their churches and ministries. The day before our meetings, four young men came to the little hotel where I and several ministry partners were staying. I soon found out they were all evangelists and were about to go back to Sudan. They spoke of their home villages and how many of their family members and friends were killed during their country's civil war, which lasted many years.

I talked with these four men for a while, and then I asked if they would like a Coke or Sprite. They all began to look at each other with surprise, and one of them, John, raised his eyebrows in excitement. I

John Singing

later learned they had never had a soft drink before.

The next day, these four guys came to our meeting. As I talked further with John, I began to hear his story through an interpreter. John was twenty years old. He had gotten married at the age of seventeen and could not pay his dowry of a mere forty dollars. He was a refugee and had no job. To him, forty dollars seemed like a million. After one year of marriage, John's wife gave birth to their son. However, during her pregnancy and labor, John was not allowed to be with her. In fact, he had not been allowed to see his own child since the birth. At the time we spoke, his son was a year and a half old. You see, in African culture, the man pays the dowry to the woman's family. This dowry could be in the form of a cow, a few chickens, or money. In John's case, it was money that was demanded. Unfortunately, he could not pay it, so he could not take his bride from her parents' home.

As I talked to John, I could hear his pain and sense his love for his family and desire to be united with them. I realized at once that

I should help. I told him later in the day that I represent American Christians who are concerned about the body of Christ in Africa and, specifically, Sudan. I told him we could help him be united with his family so he could return to Sudan and start his own church. I gave the money to the local leader to make sure that the payment of the dowry would be carried out.

Then something happened that I will never forget. John got on the ground and kissed my feet in gratitude. He realized that his dowry would be paid and he could be united with his wife and see his son for the first time.

A few years later, I was back in the refugee camps teaching at a pastors conference. As I arrived in the building, a man came running toward me with a big smile. It was John. We threw our arms around each other and embraced. He told me he heard of my coming and walked several days from Sudan to see me. He and his wife were together and happily married. His son was doing well, and they now had a second child.

I will never lose sight of what a mere forty dollars can do.

I grew up around wealth in suburban America. Some of my childhood friends' families had private jets and second and third homes. I remember as a boy in grade school flying with one of my friends on his family's private jet to go skiing in Colorado for the weekend. Just for the weekend! *This is normal*, I thought. *I'm sure most kids get to do this kind of thing.* I soon realized that most do not. Although I saw images and heard people tell stories of how people suffered around the world, I was mostly blinded to poverty.

I really thought that everyone was all right and managed to get by okay. I was sucked into a consumer culture that said to me, "Buy more and consume more and you will be happy." In truth, everyone living in North America gets caught up in the consumer mindset to some degree, and it is hard to break the power of this lie.

Another lie that I learned quickly was, "Possessions are good to accumulate. Toys are a necessity, both for children and adults." As I grew up, I slowly began to realize the sad truth. These "lessons" about consumption and possessions are actually a reflection of America's closely held values today. We have become a nation obsessed with consuming and possessing, not freedom and justice for all. I heard one time that the money spent on storage garages in North America exceeds the GNP of many countries in the world. Wow! We spend more to store our *excess* belongings than the total value of all the goods and services produced in some countries.

SLAVES TO RICHES?

Many people think that one has to have wealth to be a slave to it. But the simple fact is that you don't have to be rich to be a slave to riches. The poor can be a slave to wealth just as much as the rich. The core of the matter is not the size of our portfolio, our ability to retire by the age of forty-five, or the kind of car we drive. The real issues revolve around these questions: Are our hearts pure? Are we devoted to Jesus and His purposes around the world? Is our commitment to invest in the kingdom of God greater than our commitment to our own financial security and wealth?

Jesus calls us to be a slave to Him (see Matthew 16:24-25). The whole goal of spiritual formation is that our obedience and loyalty rests in Jesus and in His purposes on the earth, just as He taught in the Scriptures. It has become too easy to take for granted the abundance we enjoy while billions on our planet live without the basic necessities of life.

I was in Egypt and met a man with a crooked arm. When I asked what had happened, he explained that he'd broken it at a young age, and it was never set properly because he had no access to medical care. Mahatmas Gandhi said, "The world has enough for every man's need, but not enough for every man's greed."[1] Now, the need Gandhi was referring to was not the need for a vacation in the Caymans or U2's latest CD but the basic needs of survival for any human being: food, water, shelter, and proper medical care. I have traveled to more than seventy nations and have seen human suffering in some of the poorest regions on our globe. It is always interesting to hear people's opinions of poverty when they see it firsthand. I have heard comments like this: "Jesus said we will always have the poor with us, so why do anything?" and, "Why do people suffer like this when there is so much wealth in the world?" and, "The poor are so much closer to God."

The fact is that poverty is often overspiritualized. Some may believe that the poor walk through life closer to God or love God more than people who are not poor. Indeed you can find Scriptures to back up this position. Jesus said, "Blessed are you who are poor, for yours is the kingdom of God. . . . But woe to you who are rich, for you have already received your comfort" (Luke 6:20,24). And consider what James wrote: "Has not God chosen those who are poor in the eyes of the world to be rich in faith and to inherit the kingdom he promised those who love him?" (2:5). On the other hand, the Bible also provides many examples of wealthy people who loved God, including Abraham, Moses, Job, David, Solomon, and Zacchaeus.

Surely this issue of whether it's better to be poor or rich in God's eyes will always be debated within the church. But the real issue isn't really about the amount of our wealth; it's about the condition of our hearts when it comes to money. To that end, allow me to suggest a few thoughts on a believer's relationship with money:

Money is an issue of discipleship. In our process of spiritual formation — becoming like Christ in our thoughts and behavior — we must always see our relationship with money as a key indicator of growth and maturity. Particularly to Americans, the definition of "success" has become tightly intertwined with obtaining more wealth and possessions. As John Caputo says, "Your soul soars only with a spike in the Dow-Jones Industrial average; your heart leaps only at the prospect of a new tax break. The devil take you. He already has. Faith in God is for lovers, for men and women of passion, for real people with a passion for something other than taking profits, people who believe in something, who hope like mad in something, who love something with a love that surpasses understanding."[2]

As Christ's disciples, we must master money for the sake of the kingdom and not let money master us. Jesus talked more about money in His teachings than any other subject, aside from the kingdom of God. And the emphasis of those teachings was never about getting rich. In fact, more often than not, it was about giving riches away.

I believe that in our own journeys we should seek out relationships with the poor and oppressed both in our own communities and around the world. Jesus said that what you have done to the poor by feeding, clothing, and loving them, you have done to Him (see Matthew 25:40). Perhaps one reason Jesus so strongly emphasized ministry to the poor is because He knew that we would meet and experience *Him* in the midst of loving and serving the poor.

Our standard of living should reflect Christ's desire for the world, not our culture's desire to consume. Many Christians in North America have added an eleventh commandment: "With every increase in my salary, my standard of living must also increase." Surely the materialism in the church in this country is appalling to God. Why is it that we all feel we have to buy things we don't even need with money we don't even have to impress people we don't even know? We consume too much and collect piles of excess stuff that does nothing for us but clog up our lives—from video games and televisions to designer clothes and two-hundred-dollar shoes. There is an estimated 850 billion dollars per year of disposable income among evangelicals in the United States.[3] We radically need a change of heart and mind in this area. Imagine how many resources could be unleashed for kingdom work if Christians reduced their luxuries.

Money is an issue of global missions and justice. Our goal as Christ followers is not just our own personal spiritual healing and growth. We are involved in the expansion and growth of the kingdom of God in the world. Jesus has clearly sent us out to make disciples of all nations (see Matthew 28:19-20). We have been sent to be salt and light in tasteless and dark cultures around the globe. We are a part of a worldwide movement of God. There still exist more than 1,800 distinct ethnic groups in the world without a church in their culture. We are to champion and speak for justice, human rights, the environment, and peace in the world.

One of the hats I wear is that of a fund-raiser. I love asking people for money. I am not asking them for money for myself or to invest in a business venture to make them more money. I am asking them to invest in the kingdom of God and to further the cause of Christ around the world. There is no greater cause than this. It bothers me how some Christians seem to look down on missionaries who have to raise their own support, while at the same time they don't mind giving their money to non-Christian causes. Some denominations hire "professional" missionaries and pay them a salary. If we are going to advance the gospel among every people group, we must explore and embrace new models of funding missions. Paul was a great fund-raiser. When he wanted to go to Spain to preach the gospel, he boldly asked the church in Rome to help him get there (see Romans 15:24).

I often meet people who resist raising money for fear they will be perceived as "beggars for God" or "wanting an easy handout" in order to be a missionary. This fear — so pervasive within the body of Christ — is from the Devil himself. Missionaries and mission organizations always have more needs than funds. What a great problem it would be if missions had more money than they could spend. Is that even possible? Consider this: Eighty percent of the world's evangelical wealth is in North America, and that total alone represents *more than enough* to fund the Great Commission.[4]

DEBT THAT CONSUMES US

Perhaps the biggest factor preventing Christians from sending more missionaries to the field and supporting mission organizations is debt.

As George Barna points out, 33 percent of U.S. born-again Christians say it is impossible for them to get ahead in life because of the financial debt they have incurred.[5]

If you are consumed with debt and feel that God is leading you to go overseas, I challenge you never to give up your dream. If God is calling you, He will make a way. First, you must seek financial counsel. Also seek counsel from your pastor and from mission leaders you know. Share your story with them and be honest about the financial obstacles you face. Then heed their advice and guidance.

Second, become financially literate. In order to be a faithful steward of the income God provides, you need to understand proper money management, investments, and the basics of how financial systems operate. Most of all, you need to know how to make money a servant of God's purposes in your life and in the world instead of remaining in the trap of being a servant to money.

If you are a student or recent college graduate who wants to go overseas but are struggling with debt, let me share with you some additional advice I learned from veteran missiologist Ralph Winter. He encourages students to distinguish between two forms of debt: consumer debt and student loans. If you have a lot of consumer debt through credit cards, then you need to delay going to the mission field until you've paid off those debts in full. You will need to find a way to reduce your monthly expenses and perhaps get a second job to pay them off. However, if your debt is in the form of student loans, Winter suggests you factor the monthly cost of these loans into your fund-raising. Most donors would be pleased to know that you received further training, in whatever field, before going to the mission field—and most would be willing to support your education efforts.[6] Of course, as I mentioned earlier, I suggest getting professional counsel on this issue before moving forward with any plan, but I agree with Winter's advice.

IT IS BETTER TO GIVE

One of the hardest spiritual disciplines to practice is giving. But giving truly is a vital means of growth and blessing in our discipleship process. "Remembering the words the Lord himself said: 'It is more blessed to give than to receive'" (Acts 20:35). However, the average donation by adults who attend U.S. Protestant churches is only about seventeen dollars a week.[7] That's less than the cost of a pizza and a movie—and nowhere close to a true tithe (10 percent of income) for most Americans.

Indeed God wants to make us all more generous givers. We cannot out-give God. What could happen if there were a revolution of generous giving among Christians of all ages? Imagine how the world would change in a single year if Christians gave a full 10 percent of their income to the advancement of God's kingdom in the world. Imagine what could happen if those who were able gave 15, 20, or even 50 percent or more of their income to the cause of Christ. It is not unreasonable to expect that such a revolution would bring an end to hunger and disease in many nations around the world—and spark a spiritual awakening such as has not been seen since the first century AD.

How could such a revolution begin? It could begin with you. Gandhi said, "You must be the change you want to see in the world."[8]

PERHAPS GOD GIFTED YOU TO MAKE MONEY

A common misconception among Christians is that in order for them to "serve the Lord," they must walk away from what they love doing and go into full-time ministry at a church or on a campus or on the mission field. I have seen countless people pursue what others defined as "serving the Lord" and in the process forsake their true God-given talents and abilities. Let me encourage you to pursue what you are passionate about and enjoy doing. God created each of us with different skills and abilities. Perhaps going to the mission field is not what you should do, but maybe you are able to support a hundred others who should go. God has led all of us to be cocreators and comanagers with Him, and wealth creation is included in this.

The question to ask is not *How much money can I potentially make in my career?* but *How much money do I need to provide for my family's basic needs?* Then, after determining that and sticking to it, ask, *How much money can I give away to the cause of Christ through my career?* Then your purpose and motivation at work will take on a different focus. I have met people who desire to double what they give away to missions every year. What a worthy goal! You work harder to close that deal and grow your business not for a second home you don't really need but to be able to give away more toward spreading the hope of the gospel throughout the world and alleviating human suffering. As Scott Lewis, a CEO in California, says, "I am a missionary. I am using the skills and talents that God gave me to do business for the purpose of making money to fund the fulfillment of the Great Commission. . . . We get a pile of money, and we go shopping—not down at the local mall; we go shopping around the world to see where we can use this money to impact the kingdom of God. By the end of last year, we had reached $734,000 toward our goal of $1 million. . . . That is where we are tracking, and we are just thrilled."[9] Take a look at www.generousgiving.org for similar stories.

GETTING OVERSEAS THROUGH A CAREER

Perhaps you have gifts and abilities in a certain vocation and want to use that vocation to make a global impact. "What could I ever do with my accounting degree?" you may ask. The reality is you can do many things to make a strategic impact for Christ among people in the world who need to know the love of God.

A career as an accountant, engineer, or teacher can open the right door to get you overseas to places where a traditional missionary cannot go. Many are embracing the trend of sending professionals into the world to use their vocation to meet and minister to people. To learn more, ask your church leaders for information on the many programs and organizations that focus on sending professionals overseas for the cause of Christ.

A LIFE OF FAITH

The writer of Hebrews said, "Faith is being sure of what we hope for and certain of what we do not see" (11:1). All of us as Christians are called to a life of faith. The Hebrews passage goes on to say, "And without faith it is impossible to please God, because anyone who comes to him must believe that he exists and that he rewards those who earnestly seek him" (11:6). God continually wants to build and grow our faith. In fact, one way God may desire for you to grow in faith is to give up one year, two years, or your whole career to live and serve overseas among an oppressed and marginalized people group.

You don't want to settle for the American dream of independence, personal rights, and the pursuit of pleasure, safety, freedom, and security. You want something more—a life of faith that may call you to go hungry sometimes or to live without the pleasures that others have. You don't want to retire one day and then ask yourself, *Is that it? I have lived a comfortable and predictable life. But what have I really accomplished with the time I was given?* In contrast, how wonderful it would be to come to the end of your life and echo the words of the apostle Paul: "I know what it is to be in need, and I know what it is to have plenty. I have learned the secret of being content in any and every situation, whether well fed or hungry, whether living in plenty or in want. I can do everything through him who gives me strength" (Philippians 4:12-13).

It is the love of money that keeps many people from following God's call to make disciples of all nations and alleviate human suffering in the world. We make excuses, embrace lifestyles, and allow debt to consume us. Perhaps you are reading this and God's Spirit is speaking to you. You may be like the rich young ruler who Jesus told to sell all of his possessions and give the money to the poor. The young ruler's love of his possessions kept him from giving his whole life to Jesus. But what about you? What's keeping you from giving your whole life to Jesus and His kingdom?

START NOW!

In closing this chapter, I want to share a few stories from my personal experiences that I hope will inspire you to begin now to grow in the area of giving and stewardship:

A poor woman in Houston. One summer during my college years, I worked on staff in an inner-city church in Houston, Texas. One Sunday as I was locking up, a Hispanic woman asked if I could wait while she went to get her tithe for that day. I said I would, not realizing I'd be waiting for forty-five minutes while she walked home. My impatience grew along with my hunger. Finally the lady arrived, handed me the small envelope, and went on her way. I saw that it was open and looked inside and found one dime. That's right: She had made a forty-five-minute walk to get ten cents for her tithe.

Fund-raising for Indonesian outreach. Many years ago, I needed to raise three thousand dollars in just three days so I could spend eight weeks in Irian Jaya, Indonesia. I was going to be with a team working at a local Bible training school and doing ministry around the island for the summer. I didn't know how I could raise so much money in such a short period of time, but I began to pray. The next day, I went to my home church, and people began coming up to me and handing me envelopes. There were probably fifteen or twenty people who did this. The amount equaled exactly $3,100.

Eight-year-old Amy in Las Vegas. I got the following letter and was moved by the action of a young girl in Las Vegas, Nevada:

Dear Joel,

My name is Amy. About six months ago, I read your newsletter about a little girl that sent Bibles to China. I thought if she could do that, I could too!

But I mostly did it for God. I collected $915, enough to buy 305 Bibles to send through ServLife.

Sincerely,

Amy Taylor, age 8

Las Vegas, Nevada

A fund-raiser in Nepal. As I write this book, my family and I are living in Nepal. A local Nepali church we attend is building a home for the elderly in the capital city of Kathmandu. The land and building together totaled about eighty thousand dollars. The church leaders encouraged their people to give in this way: If you have a motorcycle, give five thousand rupees (about seventy dollars). If you have your own car, give twenty thousand rupees (about $275). The money has been raised! I thought this could be accomplished in America in a similar way: If you own a home, give a thousand dollars. If you have a second home, give ten thousand dollars. If you have a net worth of one million dollars or more, give fifty thousand dollars. It's a simple idea, but it could put some spice in a fund-raising project for local or global missions.

An extra BMW in Indiana. I met with a doctor for lunch, and as we talked about what it means to be a follower of Jesus, it was apparent that God was working in this man's heart regarding his material possessions. He was overwhelmed with the need for the continued growth and expansion of the gospel in the world, especially in places where churches did not even exist. It was clear to him that he needed to sell his extra BMW. He informed me of his decision to sell the car and donate the proceeds before I was able to share with him some financial needs of our ministry, not suspecting that I had been about to ask him for a donation to our mission that equaled the amount he would gain from the sale of his BMW. God does provide.

FOR REFLECTION AND DISCUSSION

1. When have you experienced someone's generosity? How did that experience inspire you?
2. Think of a time when you were moved to give your time or money to help someone in need. What is it that led you to act?
3. What did you grow up thinking about debt, and what is your perspective on it now? Do you think it is okay for Christians to be in debt? Why or why not?
4. Try this exercise with your family, small group, or Sunday school class. Give the money you collect to your church or a mission organization committed to making disciples of all nations and empowering the poor and oppressed.

- Give $5 if you have a roof over your head. $_____
- Give $1 if your house is heated. $_____
- Give $1 if you have air conditioning. $_____
- Give $2 for every bed in your house. $_____
- Give $5 for each indoor bathroom you have. $_____
- Give $1 for every phone in your house. $_____
- Give $2 for every personal computer you own. $_____
- Give $1 for every television in your house. $_____
- Give $2 for each car you own. $_____
- Give $0.01 for each item of clothing you own. $_____
- Give $0.25 for each pair of shoes you own. $_____
- Give $0.50 for every appliance you own. $_____
- Give $0.01 for every dish in your kitchen. $_____
- Give $0.50 for each meal you eat on an
  average day. $_____

- Give $0.05 for every videotape you own. $_____
- Give $0.10 for every CD and DVD you own. $_____
- Give $0.50 for every year of school you have completed. $_____
- Give $0.05 for every vitamin you take each day. $_____
- Give $0.05 for each glass of water you drink each day. $_____
- Give $0.50 for every shower you take per week. $_____
- Give $0.25 for each hour you watch TV per day. $_____
- Give $0.25 for each hour you spend online each day. $_____
- Give $1 for each load of laundry you do each week. $_____
- Give $1 for every church activity you attend each month. $_____

GRAND TOTAL $_____

chapter five

LESSONS FROM A PRAYING NUN

*If we never look at Him or think of what we owe Him and
of the death which He suffered for our sakes, I do not see how
we can get to know Him or do good works in His service. For
what can be the value of faith without works, or works which
are not united with the merit of our Lord Jesus Christ? And
what but such thoughts can arouse us to love this Lord?*

TERESA OF AVILA

*God did not make the first human because He needed
company, but because He wanted someone to whom he could
show His generosity and love. God did not tell us to follow
Him because he needed our help, but because He knew that
loving Him would make us whole.*

IRENAEUS

While a college student, I helped to organize a mission team to
Calcutta, India. I had a burning desire to experience one of the
poorest cities in the world. That might seem like a strange desire for
a college student to have, but I believe God planted it in my heart.
There was a hunger in me to understand the gospel in the context of
a culture completely foreign to my own. I suspected that some of the

ways I perceived and lived out my Christian journey had been shaped more by my American culture than by Scripture. And I really wanted to be obedient to the command of Jesus to "go and make disciples of all nations" (Matthew 28:19).

I had never been to India or organized a trip like this before, but I was thrilled at the opportunity. The city with the lowest standard of urban living in the world was our destination. In the time it took to plan the details, our team, which started with more than twenty individuals, eventually dwindled to just four. We were all young and inexperienced but ready to venture into a land that was completely alien to our understanding. Deep down, we all wanted to experience more of God than our limited suburban upbringing had shown us. We wanted to challenge the lies of the American dream, which emphasized upward mobility, income, and the acquisition of stuff. We also wanted to challenge some of the pervasive (if unspoken) Christian credos espoused by many in the West. These included such ideas as, "God wants you to be happy, comfortable, and safe" and "Being a Christian is just one aspect of your life — on the same level with your work life, your family life, or your dating life."

Many people around me taught and lived these beliefs. However, there was a "disconnect" for me between these teachings and Jesus' call for us to take up our cross and follow Him to make disciples of all nations. I could not accept that God was solely concerned with my comfort and safety. There had to be more to the Christian journey than just living the American dream by going to college, getting a job, living in the suburbs, raising a family, retiring in a warm climate, and dying.

India seemed liked a good place to sift through many of my western beliefs and presumptions. After all, India is a land of contrasts: rich and poor, urban and rural, death and life, misery and joy. It's a land of religion, temples, and a fervency of worship that truly humbled me when I saw it for the first time. People in India are not ashamed to devote themselves to idols and to ritual in their attempt to find identity, meaning, and purpose for their lives.

Just taking those first few steps out of the airport challenged my western perceptions of what life should be like. For starters, there was a cow sitting next to my taxi in front of the airport—not the most common encounter. My driver kicked it several times to get it out of the way so we could leave.

The smells that entered my nostrils were truly odors I had never experienced before. Most of them were far from pleasant or soothing. Garbage piled up along the roadways in every direction I looked. Most everyone used the street and parks as public toilets—definitely not a sight (or smell) often encountered in North America.

The day after we arrived, I decided to play a joke on my friends by telling them, "Hey, let's go visit a friend of mine." Actually I was thinking of Mother Teresa (whom I had never met), but they had no idea whom I was talking about. After many strange and doubtful looks, they agreed, and we began walking. We trekked through the city for a half hour until we came to what is called the Mother House. There was a simple sign at the door that read, "Mother Teresa."

"Your friend is Mother Teresa?" my friends asked in amazement. The joke was over shortly, however, once a nun opened the door and we humbly requested to visit Mother Teresa. We all were shocked when she said yes! Who would ever think that was possible? I thought only presidents, movie stars, and wealthy people could have an audience with the most famous nun in the world.

We were soon taken upstairs, and about five minutes later Mother Teresa came running in, full of excitement and energy.

"Welcome to India!" she said. "What brings you here?"

And then she said, "Please have one of my business cards." And she handed one to each of us.

We visited for a few minutes, and then one of the sisters came to us and said that if we wanted a photo with Mother Teresa, we

Joel with Mother Teresa in 1995

should come back the next day, as she had other guests to attend to. Of course, we did return and were immediately escorted up to the same location. She came right back out, wearing no shoes, and displaying as much energy and charisma as she did the previous day. Then she began welcoming us to India, asking what we were doing there, and handing us her business cards. It was like déjà vu. I wanted to say, "Mother, we were just here yesterday and told you who we are." But we gave her the benefit of the doubt. I later framed the business card she gave me, which she had signed with these words:

The fruit of silence is prayer
The fruit of prayer is faith
The fruit of faith is love
The fruit of love is service
The fruit of service is peace.
Mother Teresa

A few days later, our team was on a train headed toward the city of Darjeeling to minister at a school. On the train ride, I read the amazing story of Agnes Gonxha Bojaxhiu from Albania. Agnes was sixteen when she left Albania to minister in India. Long before she won the Nobel Peace Prize or received multiple honorary doctorate degrees from the most prestigious universities, this young woman heeded God's call and left her home to share Christ's love in a far-off land. When she first arrived, she took a position teaching English in a home for girls.

Sometime later, Agnes was on a train wrestling with what God was really calling her to do, and she realized He was calling her to start her own ministry to the poorest of the poor in Calcutta. When she went to her boss to ask if she could pursue this, he responded by saying, "What makes you think you can have your own ministry to the poor? You cannot even light the candles during mass."[1]

Not to be deterred, Agnes began ministering to the poor in Calcutta, and the rest of her story is known by all the world—as Agnes later changed her name to Teresa, after Saint Teresa.

I met with Mother Teresa a few more times over the next four years, but the most significant and impacting conversation I had with her was on my fourth visit to her home, at the end of 1996. I had been in Cuba earlier that year, and upon arrival in Havana, I saw two Sisters of Charity (Mother Teresa's order). They wore white saris with blue trimming and were easy to spot. I approached them and noticed that they were from India, and I thought I might practice my Hindi in Cuba. They both smiled, and we spoke for several minutes.

"What are you doing in Cuba?" one of the sisters asked.

"We are here to share Christ's love with people," I replied.

They both smiled again. I told them of my love for India and how I had met "Mother," which is the way the sisters refer to her. One of the ladies looked at me intently and said that if I go back to India, I should tell Mother that their work in Cuba is going well and they send her their greetings. I thought very little of it at the time and did not believe this conversation would come up in the future, but it did. As I said, later that year I was back in Calcutta and went to where Mother Teresa lived and worked. She was very different from the first time I had met her. She was in a wheelchair and was not the energetic woman I had met several years before.

I remembered the encounter with the sisters in Cuba and leaned over and told her I had a message for her. I said I had been in Cuba a few months before and her sisters told me to relay that their work is going well and that they send their greetings and love. She seemed to really listen to me and care what I had to say about these sisters in Cuba.

She looked up at me and asked, "Do you want to come with me to pray?"

"Of course," I replied.

A sister pushed Mother Teresa's wheelchair into a different room as I walked alongside. When we were settled, she reached out her hands to me. I extended my hands, and as she touched them, she said, "This is how we teach all our sisters to pray."

She held my hands and touched each of my fingers in turn, beginning with my left hand:

I can
I will
By God's grace
I will be
Holy

And then my right:

You
Did
It
To
Me

These words are taken from Jesus in Matthew 25:40: "The King will reply, 'I tell you the truth, whatever you did for one of the least of these brothers of mine, you did for me.'"

She then said, "You then put your hands together and pray."

We sat in a room and prayed with the other sisters for about an hour. When we had finished, Mother Teresa handed me the rosaries she'd been clutching and told me to keep them. I thought, *Wow! She gave me her rosaries!* Then I thought that she probably did not even own her own prayer beads and just wanted me to have some. Whatever the case was, I was grateful to receive them.

Mother Teresa taught me something meaningful about prayer that day: There is mystery and deep beauty to the role of prayer in the Christian life. Prayer embraces both a vertical and horizontal dimension to the Christian journey. The spiritual nurturing and growth of our lives as well as our ministry to the poor, lost, and despised are woven together like two strands of yarn. Discipleship and evangelism are married. Being and doing are somehow integrated in a holistic manner. As breathing is to the human body, prayer is essential to us as followers of Jesus, enabling us to both grow spiritually and serve others.

That day with Mother Teresa was a day that will be marked in my "spiritual memories" hall of fame. C. S. Lewis said, "Truth is not created, it is discovered." And that day, the discovery was profound. My service to others is not essential for knowing God, but my service to others is keenly linked to my growing in God.

After reflecting on a few familiar Scriptures, I realized how key the vertical and horizontal dimensions of our Christian journey really are. James says that faith without works is dead (2:17). In Ephesians 2:8, the apostle Paul explains that salvation is a gift from God. But just a few verses later, he adds that we are God's workmanship, created in Christ Jesus to do good works. Jesus says that the greatest commandment is to love God with all your heart, soul, and mind, and the second is to love your neighbor as yourself (see Matthew 22:37-39).

We will not grow and mature in our spiritual journey until we connect the vertical and horizontal. The Christian life is about how we learn to love God *and* love people. What we do in prayer and in service to others impacts our ability to grow and be transformed into the image of Jesus Christ, which is the goal of discipleship. Some people may want to just come to Christ and receive the free gift of salvation and not be concerned with giving their time, money, or energy to love people. But choosing that approach can never lead to genuine transformation, because it's only half of the equation. Jesus has called us to believe in Him *and* to do good works.

THE ROLE OF PRAYER IN TRANSFORMATION

Engaging in prayer that connects both the vertical and horizontal dimensions of the Christian life is crucial to growing and being formed into Christ's image. This sort of prayer focuses our attention on the world around us, yet it keeps us dependent on God and not our human ability. For if we rely on our human ability or intellect, then we are not truly relying on God to do in us and through us what He alone can do. There are two passages of Scripture that give us this insight:

We proclaim him, admonishing and teaching everyone with all wisdom, so that we may present everyone perfect in Christ. To this end I labor, struggling with all his energy, which so powerfully works in me. (Colossians 1:28-29)

Now to him who is able to do immeasurably more than all we ask or imagine, according to his power that is at work within us, to him be glory in the church and in Christ Jesus throughout all generations, for ever and ever! Amen. (Ephesians 3:20-21)

When I asked Mother Teresa more about prayer, she told me, "Prayer enlarges the heart until it is capable of containing the gift of God Himself." God wants us to know Him and to desire Him. Or, as A. W. Tozer stated, "God wants to be wanted."[2] All of us want to be wanted, loved, and known by someone. It is the deepest cry of the human experience. The same can be said of God. He wants people to hunger for Him as they hunger for their favorite meal after a day without eating. The unfortunate truth is that we many times don't want God. Or else we don't want the things that God wants, such as hatred of sin (see Psalms 45:7; Proverbs 8:13), justice for the poor (see Psalms 102:17; 140:12), and knowledge and worship of Him among all people and nations (see 1 Timothy 2:4; 2 Peter 3:9).

Our hearts need to change, and that change begins with prayer—and with the realization that authentic communion with God will result in the horizontal expression of humble service to others. It has always fascinated me that the one request the disciples made of Jesus was, "Lord, teach us to pray" (Luke 11:1). It was not, "Teach us how to do miracles like you do" or "Teach us how to craft a clever sermon." They learned from Jesus' example that prayer was at the center of it all: "Jesus often withdrew to lonely places and prayed" (Luke 5:16).

Many people I talk to, even church leaders, do not truly understand the essence of prayer. I was once at a pastors conference in America listening to a leader confess that he did not know how to teach on prayer. I, too, have much to learn about prayer and want to learn from the people of God who have walked before me, many of whom seem to have amazing intimacy with God through their prayer life. The lives and writings of Brother Lawrence, A. W. Tozer, Teresa of Avila, C. S. Lewis, John Wesley, Richard Foster, and Dallas Willard have all been invaluable to me. Through their examples as well as my own experience, I have learned many things about prayer. But one of the most important is this: Abundant living and fruitful ministry—no matter what kind of ministry—must be fueled and sustained through a life of prayer.

Here are some practical suggestions for ways you can nurture a sense of communion with God through prayer:

Nature. As you walk, bike, or drive, allow the beauty of God's creation to awaken your communion with the Creator. Thank Him for the beauty He created and ask Him to awaken creativity within you as you long to experience Him.

Solitude. Quietness is the basic premise of solitude and should be viewed as a doorway leading to communion with God. Times of solitude can be intentional or brought about by circumstance, such as when you are driving in the car or working on a project alone.

Silence. Søren Kierkegaard once wrote, "A man prayed, and at first he thought that prayer was talking. But he became more and more quiet until in the end he realized that prayer is listening."[3] Prayer is communication. To have effective communication between two people, one speaks and one listens, each in turn. When we learn to listen to the voice of Jesus, our prayer life will take on deeper meaning and growth. Jesus says, "My sheep listen to my voice" (John 10:27).

Art. I recall while I was in Amsterdam on a flight layover, I visited the Rikes Museum. There I observed a painting from the Renaissance that portrayed the Nativity. In the painting, all three wise men came from different nations and ethnic groups. One, of Asian descent, carried incense; another, an African, held gold; and a third, an Arab, carried myrrh. I was moved by the artist's message that from the very beginning, all nations and tribes were created to worship Jesus (see Revelation 7:9). By viewing a work of art, watching a film, or listening to a symphony, you can discover deeper truths for your Christian journey or simply be reminded of God's splendor and creativity.

Relationships. Whether in dating or marriage, relationships can be complicated and provide ample opportunity to move toward God in prayer. Healthy, nurturing relationships give us a glimpse of the way God relates to us.

Community. By having community and deepening friendships with other Christians, you can be led to pray together for each others' needs.

Work. The workplace is a mission field and provides opportunity to build relationships with people who do not know Christ. You can pray for increased wisdom on how to love colleagues the way Christ would love them.

Travel. When you travel to other countries and experience diverse cultures, your heart will be moved to deeper levels of intercession for the people you encounter. As you walk through the streets of cities and towns, you can pray for the advancement of the gospel.

Personal suffering. C. S. Lewis wrote, "God whispers in our joys, speaks to us in our conscience, but shouts to us in our pain."[4] As you experience pain in your life—through the death of someone you love, a loss of a relationship, or some other difficult circumstance—ask God to allow you to embrace the pain and use it to understand how He hurts for the lost and broken. How you approach and work through the difficult times in your life will shape how you help others heal from their pain.

Suffering of others. As you engage with people who are suffering, your compassion will be awakened and your prayer life will be deepened.

Evil. Expanding your awareness of the evil in your own society and in other societies will compel you to pray and seek God for ways to intervene and be a voice for justice and truth. Evils such as child labor, drug trafficking, genocide, and corporate greed are a few examples.

DIFFERENT WAYS TO ENGAGE IN PRAYER

Author Meister Eckhart offers wise advice when he says that styles do not bring change—rather, God does.[5] There is no magic formula to how we should pray, and we should not fall into the trap of believing that a particular method of prayer is the "right" or "best" way to bend God's ear. Recently, I was in a Hilton hotel in Cairo, Egypt, and I headed for the gift shop to buy some postcards. You would think employees of a five-star hotel would be more concerned about profit than principle—more concerned with the financial dealings of the day than matters of faith. Well, as I opened the door around four in the afternoon, I accidentally bumped a man with the door, not realizing he was standing so close. I gestured my apologies and tried to ask

Children Saying Grace at ServLife's Orphanage in North India

if the shop was open. No reply. I spoke the little Arabic I knew, hoping he would answer. Still no reply. I looked down and saw a rug on the floor in this nice shop in the Hilton. The man was preparing to pray; facing toward Mecca, he knelt on the rug, totally ignoring this young white guy who was only going to spend money in his shop. No reply. No excuse. No sale.

On another occasion, I hired a taxi to drive me from Aqaba to the capital, Amman. This is about a three- to four-hour drive through nothing but desert. After two hours in the car, with the winds gusting and the sand and the heat beating down on us, my Muslim driver stopped and asked if he could pray. I said yes, assuming he would bow his head as he sat in the front seat. But no, he got out of the car and prayed along the side of the road for fifteen minutes. This is the sort of dedication to a life of prayer that I desire.

There are many ways to pray, and nearly all of them have something of value to offer us in our spiritual journey. Here are some of the different approaches to prayer that have been meaningful to me:

Centering prayer. This is a *method* of prayer — traditionally called contemplative prayer — that prepares us to receive the gift of God's presence. It consists of responding to the Spirit of Christ by consenting to God's presence and action within. It furthers the development of contemplative prayer by quieting our hearts and minds to cooperate with the gift of God's presence.

Meditation. Simply meditating on a verse of Scripture or a word (such as *love* or *forgiveness*) has often led me into the presence of God. If I am meditating on the word *love*, for example, I ask God to show me more of His love for me, and I thank Him for the times he has shown me His love in the past. Then I begin to meditate on how I can better love others.

Lectio Divina. This Latin phrase means "into the presence of God through the text." As you read and dwell upon a particular portion of Scripture, pray that you can enter and experience the presence of God.

Prayer walking. This is exactly what it sounds like: praying while walking. You can do it alone, with a partner, or as part of a group. Perhaps you can pray Scripture together or pray for the neighborhoods and people you pass as you go your way. Prayer walking can also be an effective form of spiritual warfare in cities or countries where the people do not know God.

Repetitive phrases. Often prayerfully reciting a phrase over and over can help lead you into God's presence. You might use phrases such as "God is my refuge" or "His mercy endures forever." As you repeat these biblical truths, allow the Holy Spirit to speak to you and fill you with understanding.

The Psalms. Read, pray, and sing the psalms. Whenever I am in another country or in a church service that is in another language, I always sing along with the church, replacing the words I don't understand with the words from a psalm.

Warfare. The metaphor of war is a powerful one to think through when you are faced with impossible odds or circumstances (more about this in chapter 10).

A.C.T.S. This acronym is helpful in guiding you through different aspects of prayer. *Adoration:* Give praise to God for who He is, what He has done, and what He is going to do. *Confession:* Confess your sins and mistakes, and God, who is faithful, will hear your prayer and forgive you (see 1 John 1:9). *Thanksgiving:* Thank God for what He has done in your life, for your family, and for the blessings He has given you. *Supplication:* Pray for other people you love and know. Pray for missionaries, your church, your pastor, and the work of the church around the world.

The Lord's Prayer. Memorize, speak, and study the prayer that Jesus taught to His disciples. I often just pray this prayer to lead me into the presence of God.

"Our Father in heaven,
hallowed be your name,
your kingdom come,
your will be done
*   on earth as it is in heaven.*
Give us today our daily bread.
Forgive us our debts,
*   as we also have forgiven our debtors.*

And lead us not into temptation,
but deliver us from the evil one." (Matthew 6:9-13)

THE RESULTS OF PRAYER

Prayer is for not just our own blessing but also for the transformation of other people and nations. God hears the prayers of His people and responds accordingly. Prayer has impact! Here's what happens when we pray:

God is honored. The goal of our prayers should be that God will be exalted in every circumstance, decision, or trial so that all nations and peoples on earth will come to know Him. He said, "My name will be great among the nations, from the rising to the setting of the sun. In every place incense and pure offerings will be brought to my name, because my name will be great among the nations" (Malachi 1:11). We are often compelled to pray in hard times and stressful circumstances. However, prayer is not merely about our needs or wants but about God receiving glory throughout all the earth.

We are changed. As we see the fruit of prayer in our lives, God will change us and reveal Himself to us: "And we, who with unveiled faces all reflect the Lord's glory, are being transformed into his likeness with ever-increasing glory, which comes from the Lord, who is the Spirit" (2 Corinthians 3:18).

Families and relationships are changed. As we live a life of prayer, forgiveness happens, hurts are forgotten, and relationships are healed and transformed into healthy, vibrant, and dynamic expressions of faith. As the old saying goes, "Families that pray together stay together!"

Churches are changed. The body of Christ is made up of broken people who desire to be healed and transformed. The instrument of that healing and transformation is prayer. As Jesus said, "My house will be called a house of prayer for all nations" (Mark 11:17). As we commit to praying as individuals and families, this will overflow into our local churches. Churches will be chock-full of people who are filled with the Holy Spirit and who love, serve, and give of themselves to others.

Cities are changed. As individuals, families, and churches are transformed and live for God's glory, then their cities will change. Crime will decrease; the poor will be helped to stand on their own; neglected children will be cared for and encouraged to stay in school; widows will be served; and broken people will be loved and healed.

Nations are changed. As change happens in individuals, families, churches, and communities, whole nations will bring glory to God through administering justice and caring for the orphan and widow and the poor.

I want to close this chapter with a real-life example of the powerful impact a single person's prayer can have on a nation. In the nineteenth century, the famous missionary William Carey left England for India. His life of prayer and dedication to God served as a catalyst for major changes in Indian society. He started schools, translated the Bible and encyclopedias into local languages, helped import the printing press, and started several churches. One of the most profound impacts he made was his work to abolish the suttee. This is the Indian practice of cremating a still-living woman beside the body of her dead husband. Inspired through prayer, William Carey became a leading voice against this unjust Hindu practice. As a result of his influence, the Indian government eventually made suttee illegal.

Carey's story is impressive, but it need not be unique. Miraculous things will happen through us as well if we will simply commit ourselves to praying.

FOR REFLECTION AND DISCUSSION

1. What circumstances have you faced that have resulted in the growth of your prayer life?
2. How might your understanding of the gospel of Jesus Christ be wrongfully influenced by American culture?
3. What are two ways you can enhance your prayer life this month?
4. How are the "vertical" and "horizontal" dimensions of prayer life being expressed through your life?

chapter six

COMPASSION IS THE KEY

The "least of my brethren" are the hungry and the lonely, not
only for food, but for the Word of God; the thirsty and the
ignorant not only for water, but also for knowledge, peace,
truth, justice and love; the naked and the unloved, not only
for clothes but also for human dignity; the unwanted; the
unborn child; the racially discriminated against; the homeless
and abandoned, not only for a shelter made of bricks, but for
a heart that understands, that covers, that loves; the sick, the
dying destitute, and the captives, not only in body, but also
in mind and spirit; all those who have lost all hope and faith
in life; the alcoholics and dying addicts and all those who
have lost God (for them God was but God is) and who have
lost all hope in the power of the Spirit.

MOTHER TERESA

May I become at all times, both now and forever
A protector for those without protection
A guide for those who have lost their way
A ship for those with oceans to cross
A bridge for those with rivers to cross
A sanctuary for those in danger
A lamp for those without light
A place of refuge for those who lack shelter
And a servant to all in need.

AUTHOR UNKNOWN

He was twenty-one years old when he went to China with an upstart missionary agency.

What can I do? he asked himself. *I am so young. Everyone says I am too young to venture out to a far-off land where I've never been.*

He was not deterred by the criticism of those around him, however. He would not let his youth stop him from following God's call. He was eager to share Christ with the people of China. His compassion did not stop at mere empathy but would eventually lead him to give his life for them.

At the time he went to China, it was illegal for foreigners to enter the interior of the country. He could travel only to the port cities. But his heart was filled with so much compassion for the people of China that he ignored this law and made his way into the heart of the nation. He later wrote these words in a letter:

> *At home, you can never know what it is to be absolutely alone, amidst thousands, everyone looking on you with curiosity, with contempt, with suspicion, or with dislike. Thus to learn what it is to be despised and rejected of men . . . and then to have the love of Jesus applied to your heart by the Holy Spirit . . . this is precious, this is worth coming for.*[1]

The year was 1857, and the man was J. Hudson Taylor. We know his name today, but very few people knew of him at that early age. He was a pioneer—a young man who had a vision inspired by the Holy Spirit. Funds from home rarely arrived, but Taylor was determined to rely on God for his every need, and he never appealed to his friends in England for money. He later repeatedly told others, "Depend upon it. God's work, done in God's way, will never lack for supplies."[2]

One day a man asked Taylor to explain why he had buttons on the back of his coat. Taylor realized then that his western-style dress was distracting his listeners from the message. He then decided to dress like a Mandarin, a Chinese teacher. He was amazed at how dressing in Chinese attire allowed him to travel more freely and be accepted more readily by the people. Taylor's goal was not to have the Chinese become like English Christians but to have them become Chinese Christians.

The sufferings and hardships multiplied: Taylor's daughter died from disease; the family was almost killed in the Yangchow riot of 1868; Maria, Taylor's first wife, died during childbirth; his second wife died of cancer; sickness plagued him and his family. Yet Taylor's organization, China Inland Mission, continued its work of reaching millions for Christ.

By 1895, the mission had 641 missionaries, plus 462 Chinese helpers at 260 stations. Under Hudson Taylor's leadership, China Inland Mission supplied more than half of the Protestant missionary force in China. During the Boxer Rebellion of 1900, fifty-six of these missionaries were martyred, and hundreds of Chinese Christians were killed. The missionary work did not decline, however, and the number of missionaries quadrupled in the following decades.[3]

Compassion is absolutely essential for anyone who wants to make an impact on other people, no matter if those people are in our own communities or on the other side of the globe. For some of us, compassion comes easily. We see someone in physical or emotional pain, and we grieve for that person. For others, however, compassion does not come so easily. I am sure we all know people who respond to human suffering with apathy, giving little care for the poor, oppressed, and marginalized. When they see a starving child on television, perhaps they get angry and think, *This group puts these images on television just to make me feel bad. I have enough troubles of my own as it is. I can't be expected to solve the world's problems too.*

In the back of our mind, we all know that suffering is real in the world, but sometimes it's hard not to respond with frustration when disturbing images come spilling into our living room week after week.

What good does it really do for relief organizations to shove these images in our faces? What can we do to make a dent in the suffering that seems so pervasive across the world?

For many of us who are followers of Jesus Christ, we have missed the biblical understanding of compassion. I often meet Buddhists, Hindus, Muslims, and Jews who demonstrate more biblical compassion for the oppressed than some Christians I've met. Surely if the risen Christ lives in us, we should follow the model of Jesus and have compassion that inspires action. Biblical compassion is not merely feeling pity for someone. Anyone can feel bad about the world's problems. But as God works in us, we will desire to step out and offer practical help and comfort.

COMPASSION STARTS WITH LOOKING AND LISTENING

How do we get that kind of compassion for the lost, suffering, and oppressed? How can we grow in the kind of compassion that moves the heart of God?

We look to Jesus to see how He responded through compassion. Consider this story from His life:

A man with leprosy came to him and begged him on his knees, "If you are willing, you can make me clean."

Filled with compassion, Jesus reached out his hand and touched the man. "I am willing," he said. "Be clean!" Immediately the leprosy left him and he was cured.

Jesus sent him away at once with a strong warning: "See that you don't tell this to anyone. But go, show yourself to the priest and offer the sacrifices that Moses commanded for your cleansing, as a testimony to them." Instead he went out and began to talk freely, spreading the news. As a result, Jesus could no longer enter a town openly but stayed outside in lonely places. Yet the people still came to him from everywhere. (Mark 1:40-45)

In this familiar story, we see a beautiful model for how our compassion for others should lead us. The man with leprosy came to Jesus and spoke to Him, and at first all Jesus did was listen. He was present and aware of this man's suffering and humility. Though He may have been eager to get on with His own agenda for the day, He was willing to stop and make Himself aware of the suffering before Him. What does it mean for us to listen in this way?

On one level, "listening compassion" starts wherever we live and with whomever we come across. Whether in our home, in the classroom, or at work, we can listen to those who express their pain or perhaps hide their pain behind their busyness or a forced smile. Only through listening in this way can our compassion be awakened. If we do not have a heart for the lost and the poor, it means we are not looking and listening intently enough.

This "listening compassion" can also extend to the world at large. The events of September 11, 2001, were a clear indication for all Americans on this issue. It was interesting to see a pattern develop among different parts of the country and different generations toward the horrible terrorist attack. Some became more patriotic and wanted to buy more American flags to hang on their front porches or on their car antennas. Others became more curious and wanted to understand why so much hatred toward America exists. Some just asked, "Who did this?" while others asked, "Why did this happen?" I think younger generations tended to ask the why question and become more globally aware, while the older generations became more patriotic. Others responded with greater apathy and passivity toward the world and still did not understand their role in the global community.

How can Christians become better listeners and really hear what is going on in the world? It all begins with following the model of Jesus to see and listen to those in need around us and then extending that compassion to those who live far away.

The world today is filled with suffering. The distance between the "haves" and "have nots" is growing. Poverty, disease, war, and injustice leave millions of people without access to food, water, basic health care, education, and access to the gospel. Today there are more than thirty wars going on across the globe, and there are millions of people who live with very little possibility of even meeting a Christian because there are not many around them. Here are a few brief statistics to put things in perspective:

- Forty-two million people are now living with HIV/AIDS. In Botswana alone an appalling 35 percent of the adult population is living with this disease.[4]
- More than 1 billion people live in absolute poverty. This includes 700 million people living in slums, 500 million people on the verge of starvation, 93 million beggars, and 200 million children exploited for labor.[5]
- A majority of people alive today do not know the Savior. This includes 1.19 billion Muslims, 811 million Hindus, 360 million Buddhists, 228 million ethnoreligionists, 23 million Sikhs, 14 million Jews, 768 million agnostics, and 150 million atheists.[6]

Because we are bombarded with data and statistics every day, our minds may tend to grow numb at reading such staggering figures. But remember that each person represented in these numbers is an individual with hopes, cares, and wishes—just like you and me.

COMPASSION STIRS THE HEART

I have stood in refugee camps in Africa, garbage cities in Cairo, and among the untouchables in India, and I have been filled with pain. It does not always come. But when it does, God is speaking and present.

The Greek word for compassion is *splagchnizomai*, which means "to have the bowels yearn, i.e. (figuratively) feel sympathy, to pity."[7] The Mark passage quoted in the previous section says, "Filled with compassion, Jesus reached out his hand and touched the man" (1:41-42). For Jesus, compassion meant there was a physical reaction: He was "filled." We should pray that God fills us with compassion that allows us to be physically affected.

I remember the first time I experienced compassion on this level. I was walking through the streets in Calcutta, India. The city that is ranked with the lowest standard of urban living in the world is filled with millions of people who live on the streets. On one occasion, I found myself unable to proceed, due to the dozens of people lying on the road. They were lying in human excrement. Some looked as if they were close to death, and most were naked and malnourished. The smell and the image still haunt me to this day. My reaction was too much to process, and I began to weep as I navigated my way around this mass of suffering people. I then realized that I was across the street from one of Mother Teresa's homes for the dying. These villagers had been brought to Calcutta to Mother Teresa's home to receive comfort and dignity as they died.

God created emotion for a reason, but some believers don't recognize—or use—this gift for what it is. I see two mistakes made in this area. First, for whatever reason, many of us do not integrate our emotions with our faith. We might have heard that choosing Jesus should not be an emotional decision. We then seem to separate emotion from our faith and live out our beliefs in only a cognitive, pragmatic, and rational way. We are fine with and affirmed in exercising our emotions in other areas of our lives: getting angry at our golf game, crying at a movie, or laughing at a sitcom. But when it comes to using our emotion in a way that moves us to commitment or action in our faith, we are often hesitant.

Another mistake we can make is the opposite extreme. We place too much emphasis on our emotions and refuse to take action unless we "feel like it." I have heard many times, "I don't read my Bible because I don't feel like it." Or, "I didn't share my faith with my friend because it didn't feel right." We know clearly through Scripture that God wants us to study His Word and be active in sharing our faith whether we feel like it or not (see Philemon 6). God created all of us as emotional beings, and He wants to use our emotion to lead us to actions that might seem foolish to the world but will bring honor to God.

COMPASSION ALWAYS PROMPTS ACTION

I overheard a comment in which a man was talking about his friend's compassionate spirit: "Susan really has a lot of compassion for her friend, because she really is sad for her all the time."

Well, that's part of the equation. Biblical compassion, however, is more than just a feeling. It provokes us to action. As Jesus demonstrates in the story of healing the leper, true compassion leads us to do something to alleviate the suffering we see. What action we take depends on our gifts and will be different for all of us. For some it will mean leaving a mundane and unfulfilling job and moving to another culture to give the love of Jesus Christ to those who desperately need it. For some it will mean selling a second home or other luxuries to free up money to give to the cause of Christ. For others it will mean becoming an intercessor and committing to pray for the advance of the gospel and the church in the world.

I recently came across a ministry in Kathmandu, Nepal, that filled me with hope and inspiration. Nepal provides no kind of government help to the handicapped. Most of them are outcasts, as the majority Hindu population views them as "cursed" by the gods or believes they did a bad deed in their former life. But an Indian man has gathered about thirty-five disabled people to live in his "Prayer Tower," as they call it. These disabled men and women have come to this ministry center solely to pray. Twenty-four hours a day, seven days a week, they take two-hour shifts and continually lift up prayers to God. All of the people I talked to there said something like, "My life is filled with purpose now. My compassion for my country is being put into action because now I can do something about it." No one is incapable of acting out of compassion.

COMPASSION IS CONCERNED WITH HELPING THE "WHOLE" PERSON

Biblical compassion does not merely offer help to someone once and then leave them to their own devices after that. Jesus was not only concerned with healing the leper's disease; He was concerned with his life as a whole. I believe we can learn two lessons from Jesus when it comes to using our compassion in a productive way.

Spiritual restoration. First and foremost we should be concerned that people are spiritually restored to God through Christ. As the apostle Peter wrote, "the Lord is not slow in keeping his promise, as some understand slowness. He is patient with you, not wanting anyone to perish, but everyone to come to repentance" (2 Peter 3:9). We must realize that God wants every person in our school, office, family, and the world to know Jesus Christ as Lord and Savior. This is the greatest gift we as followers of Christ have to offer. We cannot act with compassion without remembering Peter's words, "Be prepared to give an answer to everyone who asks you to give the reason for the hope that you have. But do this with gentleness and respect" (1 Peter 3:15).

Societal restoration. There are societal implications when it comes to living out the gospel. When our compassion leads us to help orphans in the world, it is not enough to simply share the message of Christ with them verbally. Compassion compels us also to see that they are loved, fed, clothed, and educated. In the same way, when our compassion leads us to love victims of HIV/AIDS, we are prompted to create ways for victims to be cared for so they can become productive members of their communities. Of course, exactly what it looks like to help someone experience societal restoration will change depending on the person and the circumstance. There is no one "answer" for everyone. We must follow the leading of the Holy Spirit and seek counsel from others. Imagine the different implications of bringing restoration to diverse groups such as convicts, orphans, drug addicts, prostitutes, college graduates, children, or an unreached nomadic people group with no nation-state of their own.

I love what James writes:

> *What good is it, my brothers, if a man claims to have faith but has no deeds? Can such faith save him? Suppose a brother or sister is without clothes and daily food. If one of you says to him, "Go, I wish you well; keep warm and well fed," but does nothing about his physical needs, what good is it? In the same way, faith by itself, if it is not accompanied by action, is dead.*
>
> *But someone will say, "You have faith; I have deeds."*
>
> *Show me your faith without deeds, and I will show you my faith by what I do. You believe that there is one God. Good! Even the demons believe that—and shudder. (2:14-19)*

What James means is that we must be holistic in our compassion. We should not simply preach the gospel without loving people in practical ways.

C. T. Studd's motto was, "Some wish to live within the sound of the Church or Chapel bell; I want to run a Rescue Shop within a yard of hell." He was twenty-four when, in 1885, his compassion for the poor and lost made him leave for China to join Hudson Taylor. Like Taylor,

Studd did not let his age stop him from serving Jesus and giving his whole life in service to God. His compassion did more than cause him to feel sorry for the people around the world—it provoked him to action.

Others told him that he was too young to go to China. Many said, "What do you have to offer? You are just a young man." But he knew God was calling and that he must obey.

Some time later, Studd's father died and left him a large inheritance, which he chose to give to the English evangelist and social activist George Mueller, who was running orphanages and other ministries. Concerning that choice, Studd later wrote, "If Jesus Christ be God and died for me, then no sacrifice can be too great for me to make for Him."

Eventually he left China to minister in India and Sudan, which was the largest unreached area of the world at that time. Many accused Studd of being *too* zealous for God. To that he replied, "How could I spend the best years of my life in living for the honors of this world, when thousands of souls are perishing every day?"[8]

That's the kind of motto—and compassion—we can all live by.

FOR REFLECTION AND DISCUSSION

1. Does compassion come easily for you? Why or why not?
2. What is the most profound or memorable moment in which you experienced compassion for a person or group of people? Describe it.
3. How can you develop more compassion in your Christian journey?
4. What are some other moments in the life of Jesus in which He exercised compassion?
5. Where else in the Bible can you find powerful examples of compassion in action?

chapter seven

THE WAY UP IS DOWN

*The great paradox which Scripture reveals to us is that real
and total freedom can only be found through downward
mobility. . . . The divine way is indeed the downward way.*

HENRI NOUWEN

*No one can get up to that far crest unless he first goes down
to the valley below. For our way leads downward. . . . Christ
showed this himself.*

AUGUSTINE OF HIPPO

I have led an unorthodox life ever since I graduated from college. The
phrase "shallow tent pegs" best described my life as a single man and
describes it as a family man today. In 2004 alone, my wife, son, and
I lived in four cities in three different nations. So you can imagine as
a single man, up to the age of twenty-nine, I was highly mobile and
constantly traveling in order to do ministry around the world.

As you might expect, meeting my wife, our dating experience,
and our engagement were all pretty unorthodox as well. Elise and
I met in Orlando at a conference where we had both been asked to
speak. Although we did not start to date until a few months later, I
immediately recognized that she had a heart for Jesus and the world
unlike anyone else I had met. I was content being single, and most

of my family and close friends thought I would stay that way for the rest of my life. At the very least, because of my lifestyle, I knew that God would have to work in miraculous ways to bring me a soul mate. Our dating and engagement all happened long-distance. I moved to Colorado just three days before we were to get married. It is not the sort of courtship process I would recommend to anyone else, but it is how it happened for us.

At one point during our engagement, I went to visit Elise in Colorado and she began to complain about extreme pain in her side. When the pain increased, I decided to take her to the emergency room, fearing it was her appendix. Upon examination, the doctors found an eight-centimeter cyst on one of her ovaries. After more tests, her doctor told her the news no patient wants to hear: "You will need to go to the cancer center for tests because there is a chance that the cyst is malignant."

So my fiancée and I made visits to a Denver cancer center anticipating the surgery to remove the cyst. This painful and stressful time came to a climax one evening as she looked up and asked me, "If I do have cancer and they say I only have one year to live, do you still want to get married?"

I could not believe the question nor the circumstance we found ourselves facing. It was the kind of situation you read about in books; it seemed unreal. I looked at Elise and said, "I love you and want to marry you even if we get to spend just one year together."

Thankfully, the cyst was successfully removed, and there was no cancer. However, during the surgery the doctor punctured her bladder, and as a result, she had to be fitted with a catheter to drain off her fluids while the bladder healed. That was just two weeks before our wedding.

For those who don't know what this device is, it is a small bag to hold urine and is usually used by elderly people. We did not know whether it was going to be removed before our wedding day. There was so much unknown, and we were both fearful about what might happen. The day we had waited for our whole lives would be very challenging with this device, which Elise had to have strapped to her leg everywhere she went.

Even so, God used this period of hardship and pain during our engagement to grow and mature us in our relationship with Him and in our love and commitment to each other. With characteristic humor, Elise said to me several days before the wedding, "We have a ring bearer. Now we just need to find a catheter bearer for the ceremony." Thankfully, the doctors were able to remove the catheter just a few days before we walked down the aisle. I was one happy man!

SUFFERING PRODUCES GROWTH

Often Christians see suffering as an unwanted obstacle to their spiritual growth in Christ. Or perhaps they believe suffering comes upon them as punishment for some wrong they have done. Despite the adversity Elise and I experienced during our engagement, we both now clearly see how God brought us together through that experience.

Some see suffering as meaningless and believe that nothing beneficial can come from it. However, God often uses these times more than any other to grow and mature us in our spiritual journey. Typically we in the West want a "happy" Christianity that is free of all suffering and pain. Our prayers are filled with this kind of thinking: "Lord, keep us safe. . . . Make us prosperous. . . . Help us be successful." As I travel throughout the western church, I hear these kinds of prayers often. I always find myself thinking, *These are nice prayers, but are they really biblical?*

I once heard Dr. Tony Campolo relate his experience of asking parents in Japan what they wanted for their children. They said, "We want our children to be successful." He later asked Italian parents the same question, and they responded, "We want our children to be good." But when he asks American parents what they want for their children, they usually respond, "We want them to be happy and safe." (I, too, have asked this question of people from different cultures around the world. When I ask people from India, they say they want their children to be "noble." When I ask Koreans, they say "diligent." When I ask Thai people, they say "hard workers.")

If we're honest about our desires, we will realize that many of us in the West want the "good life" for our children and for ourselves — a life free from all pain, hurt, and suffering. However, that sort of life is not reality, and no one will ever find it this side of heaven. Just as you can't avoid getting wet if you jump in the ocean, so you cannot live a life without suffering and pain.

When did Jesus ever promise happiness or safety for those who choose to follow Him? I have had people say to me, "I am really suffering through this situation, and I just don't understand why God allowed it to happen. I don't see any way this experience can help me learn or grow." In reality, hardship is one of the most effective tools God uses to help us grow and mature into the kind of people He wants us to be.

Throughout Scripture we see how God uses suffering to transform and mature people into Christlikeness. The apostle Peter wrote, "Dear friends, do not be surprised at the painful trial you are suffering, as though something strange were happening to you. But rejoice that you participate in the sufferings of Christ, so that you may be overjoyed when his glory is revealed" (1 Peter 4:12-13). Whatever circumstance causes pain in our lives, God wants us to embrace that pain and let Him use it to grow us in our faith rather than run from it or pretend it doesn't exist.

Do you know people who are really good at giving you the "right" answer rather than the "real" answer? Often we ask others, "How are you?" and the response is as superficial as it is automatic: "Fine, just fine." To ignore your pain or to live in denial of it is not good. We should be honest with our pain but also use discernment and wisdom in choosing with whom we share our struggles. I have often seen people further injured after being vulnerable or overly honest with someone they did not know well or who was not mature enough to genuinely listen to their struggle.

UNDERSTANDING PARADOX IN SCRIPTURE

You will find many paradoxes throughout Scripture, and all of them, though seeming to be self-contradicting, are actually true to the core. Life is filled with mystery, paradox, and parable. It is not all meant to fit into nicely organized categories and solutions. Scientists tell us that we use less than 10 percent of our brains to understand the basic facts of our world—things like 2 + 2 = 4, and water boils at one hundred degrees Celsius. The other 90 percent of our brain, scientists say, exists to wrestle with mystery and paradox.

In reading the Bible one soon finds that paradox is everywhere. For example, the Scriptures tell us that if you want to live, you must first die. "I have been crucified with Christ and I no longer live, but Christ lives in me. The life I live in the body, I live by faith in the Son of God, who loved me and gave himself for me" (Galatians 2:20). Jesus also says that if you really want to find your life, you must first lose it (see Matthew 16:25) and if you want to be exalted, you must humble yourself (see Matthew 23:12). In our spiritual journeys, often the way up is to first go down.

DEATH LEADS TO LIFE

What will bring about the continued growth of the church in the world? How will the church expand into regions where it does not yet exist? Surely it will be when the people of God around the world respond and choose to live among ethnic groups that have few or no

Christian witnesses. We should have the same ambition as Paul: "to preach the gospel where Christ was not known, so that I would not be building on someone else's foundation" (Romans 15:20).

However, it will not be through our strategy or our clever ideas that the world is won, but through our blood. The early church father Tertullian said, "The Blood of the Martyrs is the seed of the church." This means that wherever the blood of Christians has been shed, the church has grown. History proves this fact. Yes, strategy, wisdom, and planning are crucial, but they cannot replace the deeper reality that it is the very blood of people's lives that will prepare the soil for people to hear and believe the gospel.

One of the first missionaries to Korea was Robert J. Thomas. He was ordained on June 4, 1863, at a little church in Hanover, Wales. He and his wife left in July, sent by the London Missionary Society, and soon arrived at Shanghai, China. Thomas's wife died not long after their arrival. In 1866, having evangelized for a few months in Korea and studied the language, Thomas sailed with the American ship *General Sherman* along the Taedong River (where the capital of North Korea is today). The *General Sherman* became grounded on a sandbar.

The Korean soldiers on shore were suspicious and scared. They forced the crew to abandon ship, then set upon the sailors with long knives. When Thomas saw that he was going to be killed, he held out the Korean Bible to them, saying, "Jesus, Jesus." They cut off his head.

Twenty-five years after Thomas's death, someone discovered a little guesthouse in that same area with some strange wallpaper. The paper had Korean characters printed on it. The owner of the house explained that he had pasted the pages of a book on the wall to pre-serve the writing. Many of the guests — as well as the owner — would "read the walls." This was the Bible that Thomas had thrust toward his murderers. Today it is said that South Korea is more than 30 percent

Christian, perhaps more. I believe it was the heart and boldness of Robert Thomas that paved the way for others to carry the gospel to that land. He willingly gave his life so others would have a chance to hear the gospel of Jesus Christ.

I have preached in Korea several times. I always ask Korean pastors what caused the amazing growth of the church in South Korea over the past fifty years. The answer is always the same: "Prayer and the blood of the missionaries who brought the gospel to us." Jesus said, "I tell you the truth, unless a kernel of wheat falls to the ground and dies, it remains only a single seed. But if it dies, it produces many seeds" (John 12:24). Jesus was talking about His own death in this passage, illustrating that His death was necessary to establish His kingdom. His disciples thought He was going to establish an earthly kingdom. But it was only through the death of Jesus that the will of God would be done.

I believe that the reason many areas of the world have very few Christians is that we are not willing to go at any cost and shed our own blood or allow the blood of our children to be shed for Christ's sake. The well-known Christian martyr Jim Elliot wrote, "He is no fool to give up what he cannot keep, in order to gain what he cannot lose."[1]

PERSECUTION IN THE FIRST-CENTURY CHURCH

Acts 1:8 is a famous verse used to explain the purpose of the church, both locally and globally. After Jesus' resurrection, He said to His disciples, "But you will receive power when the Holy Spirit comes on you; and you will be my witnesses in Jerusalem, and in all Judea and Samaria, and to the ends of the earth." (The Greek word translated "witness" here is *martus*.[2] The English word *martyr* is also derived from this Greek word.)

According to the classic book *Foxe's Book of Martyrs*, all of Jesus' apostles except John faced a martyr's death—along with hundreds of other first-century believers. This is said to be one of the greatest evidences of the resurrection of Jesus. If Jesus had not been raised from the dead, why would all these followers so willingly lay down their lives for Him? Among those who faced execution for the cause of Christ are the following:

Stephen, whose story is recorded in the book of Acts (see 6–7), was the first martyr. He was cast out of the city and stoned to death. His death marked the beginning of severe persecution that arose against all who professed belief in Christ as the Messiah. Luke tells that "a great persecution broke out against the church at Jerusalem, and all except the apostles were scattered throughout Judea and Samaria" (Acts 8:1). About two thousand Christians—including Nicanor, another of the seven deacons chosen in Acts 6:5—suffered martyrdom during the persecution that arose after Stephen's murder.

James was the elder brother of John and a relative of Jesus. His death took place ten years after Stephen's. According to *Foxe's Book of Martyrs*:

> *The account given us by an eminent primitive writer, Clemens Alexandrinus, ought not to be overlooked; that, as James was led to the place of martyrdom, his accuser was brought to repent of his conduct by the apostle's extraordinary courage and undauntedness, and fell down at his feet to request his pardon, professing himself a Christian, and resolving that James should not receive the crown of martyrdom alone. Hence they were both beheaded at the same time. Thus did the first apostolic martyr cheerfully and resolutely receive that cup, which he had told our Savior he was ready to drink. Timon and Parmenas suffered martyrdom about the same time; the one at Philippi, and the other in Macedonia. These events took place A.D. 44.[3]*

Philip was scourged, thrown into prison, and crucified in AD 54.

Matthew was slain with a halberd in the city of Nadabah in AD 60.

James, who was ninety-four at the time of his martyrdom, was beaten and stoned by the Jews and finally had his brains dashed out with a fuller's club.

Matthias, of whom less is known than of most of the other disciples, was elected to fill the vacant place of Judas. He was stoned at Jerusalem and then beheaded.

Andrew, the brother of Peter, preached the gospel to many Asian nations. But upon his arrival at Edessa, he was taken and crucified on a cross.

Mark was dragged through the streets by the people of Alexandria until he died.

Peter was condemned to death and crucified in Rome. He was crucified upside down at his own request because he insisted he was unworthy to be crucified in the same manner as the Lord.

Paul, after his great missionary journeys, fell under persecution by Nero. The Roman emperor had Paul taken out of the city and killed with a sword.

Jude, the brother of James, was commonly called Thaddeus. He was crucified at Edessa in AD 72.

Bartholomew was beaten and then crucified.

Thomas preached the gospel in India. His message incited the rage of the pagan priests, and he was martyred by being thrust through with a spear.

Luke, the author of the gospel that bears his name, traveled with Paul through various countries. He is said to have been hanged on an olive tree by the idolatrous priests of Greece.

Simon preached the gospel in Mauritania, Africa, and finally in Britain, where he was crucified in AD 74.

Barnabas's death is supposed to have been the result of stoning in Cyprus in AD 73.

John, the "beloved disciple," was cast into a cauldron of boiling oil. He escaped by miracle, without injury. Domitian afterward banished him to the Isle of Patmos, and that is where he wrote the book of Revelation. Nerva, the successor of Domitian, recalled him from exile. He was the only apostle who escaped a violent death.

GLOBAL PERSECUTION TODAY

Christian persecution did not end in the first century, of course. It has continued to impact the church throughout the centuries, from the time of the original disciples right up to the present. Missiologists estimate that in the twentieth century alone, more Christians were martyred than in all the previous centuries combined.[4] It is important to understand that the problem that lies before us is nothing new. In more than sixty countries, according to an official U.S. State Department report, Christians face the reality of massacre, rape, torture, mutilation, family division, harassment, imprisonment, slavery, and discrimination in education and employment.[5] According to the organization The International Day of Prayer for the Persecuted Church, about 200 million Christians around the world face overt persecution, and another 350 million face various forms of discrimination and restrictions.[6]

While visiting with pastors from Sudan in refugee camps in Uganda, I was stunned to discover that every one of them had a unique story of religious persecution. All had suffered injustice at the hands of others because of their faith in Christ or their leadership role in the church. The stories ranged from a church being burned to a finger being chopped off. One man told that his church members were thrown into an empty well and had gasoline poured over them. They were set on fire, and the pastor was forced to watch them burn to death. Another man told me of the time a revolver had been put to his head with just one bullet in the cylinder. The trigger was pulled, and he was forced to endure the mental torture of not knowing if it would go off.

Though each of those pastors had suffered, there was evident calm and forgiveness in their hearts. They all expressed desire to go back to share the love and forgiveness of Jesus with their oppressors. It was an experience I will never forget. I am certain many crowns await these men in heaven.

Here's a quick overview of just some of the "hot spot" regions of the world, where persecution is especially strong today:

Nepal. There is still an anti-conversion law in the constitution. People can face seven years in prison if they convert to Christianity.

Parts of India. Hindu nationalism rises against both Christians and Muslims. Hindu zealots often beat those of other faiths, publicly ridicule them, and prevent them from getting jobs.

Egypt. Muslim attacks against Coptic Christians are common and are not being effectively countered by the government. The government, in fact, is often complicit in the persecution, as it frequently restricts expansion and even repair of Christian facilities by withholding building permits.

Iran. Converting from Islam to another faith is a criminal offense. Christians are routinely threatened, arrested, imprisoned, and tortured because of their faith.

Nigeria. Nigeria is a religiously divided country; Christians are located primarily in the south, while the north is largely Muslim. The government appears to be conducting a campaign to eradicate all evidence of Christianity in the northern part of the country. Church burning is common.

North Korea. The entire country is suffering from a devastating famine; starvation and near-starvation are common. Even with this overshadowing struggle, however, Christians are still regularly persecuted and imprisoned for their beliefs.

Pakistan. Christians have frequently been the target of

trumped-up charges of blasphemy. Believers are often the target of violent mobs of fundamentalist Muslims. A high-court judge who had the courage to acquit Christians in one blasphemy case was subsequently assassinated.

Saudi Arabia. Christians are forbidden to worship, even within the U.S. embassy. Muslim citizens who convert to Christianity are subject to the death penalty.

Vietnam. The Vietnamese government requires all religious groups to register. But since the civil war ended in the mid-1970s, no Protestant group has been granted official recognition. The government rigidly controls the Catholic church by placing official restrictions on the number of students permitted in seminaries, restricting the number of ordinations allowed by law, and several other similar anti-Christian regulations.

THE BIBLICAL PERSPECTIVE ON PERSECUTION

In order to truly understand why persecution against Christians exists in the world today and how we should respond to it, we must examine this important theme from a biblical perspective. Here are a few key Scriptures you can use to begin your own exploration. As you study the Word, watch for other verses that teach on the issue of suffering for your faith.

The Bible says, "Everyone who wants to live a godly life in Christ Jesus will be persecuted" (2 Timothy 3:12). However, you should not let this news discourage you from following Jesus with your whole heart, because the Bible also speaks clearly of the heavenly rewards awaiting us for the suffering we endure in this life: "Blessed is the man who perseveres under trial, because when he has stood the test, he will receive the crown of life that God has promised to those who love him" (James 1:12).

The Bible also lists several benefits of suffering that come to us on this side of heaven. One of the most important of these is spiritual maturity: "Consider it pure joy, my brothers, whenever you face trials of many kinds, because you know that the testing of your faith develops perseverance. Perseverance must finish its work so that you may be mature and complete, not lacking anything" (James 1:2-5).

We can also take comfort in knowing that when Jesus returns, God will bring justice to those who persecute Christians: "All this is evidence that God's judgment is right, and as a result you will be counted worthy of the kingdom of God, for which you are suffering. God is just: He will pay back trouble to those who trouble you" (2 Thessalonians 1:5-6).

We should not fear death as followers of Jesus. Perhaps it is natural to fear the manner in which we will die or the pain we may suffer before death. However, death for the Christian is merely the doorway to heaven and the presence of God. It is not the end. I am amazed at how many Christians I talk to who fear death. The apostle Paul wrote,

> *Now we know that if the earthly tent we live in is destroyed, we have a building from God, an eternal house in heaven, not built by human hands. Meanwhile we groan, longing to be clothed with our heavenly dwelling, because when we are clothed, we will not be found naked. For while we are in this tent, we groan and are burdened, because we do not wish to be unclothed but to be clothed with our heavenly dwelling, so that what is mortal may be swallowed up by life. . . . We live by faith, not by sight. We are confident, I say, and would prefer to be away from the body and at home with the Lord. So we make it our goal to please him, whether we are at home in the body or away from it. (2 Corinthians 5:1-4,7-9)*

God uses persecution and trials for his purposes. His purpose is that all people on the earth will worship Him and know Him through faith in Jesus Christ. Persecution solidifies within our hearts a genuine faith that glorifies Jesus Christ. The Bible says, "These [sufferings] have come so that your faith—of greater worth than gold, which perishes even though refined by fire—may be proved genuine and may result in praise, glory and honor when Jesus Christ is revealed" (1 Peter 1:7). What's more, persecution also reveals Jesus Christ in us. Once again, Paul addressed this:

> But we have this treasure in jars of clay to show that this all-surpassing power is from God and not from us. We are hard pressed on every side, but not crushed; perplexed, but not in despair; persecuted, but not abandoned; struck down, but not destroyed. We always carry around in our body the death of Jesus, so that the life of Jesus may also be revealed in our body. For we who are alive are always being given over to death for Jesus' sake, so that his life may be revealed in our mortal body. (2 Corinthians 4:7-11)

Suffering encourages others to be more courageous in their testimony. When you see others being persecuted for their faith in Christ, their example inspires you to become more bold and confident in sharing your own faith. The Bible says,

> Now I want you to know, brothers, that what has happened to me has really served to advance the gospel. As a result, it has become clear throughout the whole palace guard and to everyone else that I am in chains for Christ. Because of my chains, most of the brothers in the Lord have been encouraged to speak the word of God more courageously and fearlessly. (Philippians 1:12-14)

Finally, persecution does something amazing in that it actually spreads the gospel to other places. We've already seen how early believers were "scattered throughout Judea and Samaria" (Acts 8:1) following Stephen's death. And what did those believers do when they fled for safety in other areas? "Those who had been scattered preached the Word wherever they went" (Acts 8:4). Persecution often has the opposite effect than the one intended by the instigators: The gospel advances and believers embolden.

THE BIBLICAL RESPONSE TO PERSECUTION

There are numerous examples in the Bible to help us understand how we should respond to persecution:

We should remember the persecuted as if we ourselves were suffering: "Remember those in prison as if you were their fellow prisoners, and those who are mistreated as if you yourselves were suffering" (Hebrews 13:3).

We should stand side by side with the persecuted believers around the world and even accept personal loss in order to support them:

> *Remember those earlier days after you had received the light, when you stood your ground in a great contest in the face of suffering. Sometimes you were publicly exposed to insult and persecution; at other times you stood side by side with those who were so treated. You sympathized with those in prison and joyfully accepted the confiscation of your property, because you knew that you yourselves had better and lasting possessions. (Hebrews 10:32-34)*

We should encourage other Christians with the stories of faith and endurance we hear about. Paul wrote, "Therefore, among God's churches we boast about your perseverance and faith in all the persecutions and trials you are enduring" (2 Thessalonians 1:4). Paul boasted to other Christians about the persecution the believers in Thessalonica endured as they followed Jesus Christ.

We should take action to rescue the persecuted: "Rescue those being led away to death; hold back those staggering toward slaughter" (Proverbs 24:11). Many times we have the tendency to respond to those who are persecuted in other lands solely by praying for them. While this is good, the Bible says we should show as much concern as we would if the persecuted ones lived in our own community. We are all a part of the same family. "If one part suffers, every part suffers with it; if one part is honored, every part rejoices with it" (1 Corinthians 12:26).

We should love and pray for the ones who are persecuting believers. This is much easier said than done. But as Jesus instructed, "You have heard that it was said, 'Love your neighbor and hate your enemy.' But I tell you: Love your enemies and pray for those who persecute you" (Matthew 5:43-44). As you pray for those who persecute the church, remember who the true enemy is. Paul tells us in the book of Ephesians, "For our struggle is not against flesh and blood, but against the rulers, against the authorities, against the powers of this dark world and against the spiritual forces of evil in the heavenly realms" (6:12).

Sudan is a region where Christians have been killed for their faith and ministry for Jesus. It is also a place where the church has grown through this persecution. Joseph Oloya Hakim is a ServLife missionary in Africa. He is from Sudan and has personally witnessed great atrocities against Christians, many of whom have been put to death for their faith. Reflecting on the reality of persecution and its true source, he writes,

We here are in exile from our mother land, Sudan. We persevere and strive for maturity wherever we live. I believe effective Christian maturity is not so much a goal to be achieved, but rather a lifestyle to be developed. From all points on the compass, all along the line of battle, in the vanguard and in the rear, at dawn of the day and in the midnight hour, Satan hinders us. If we toil in the fields, he seeks to break the ploughshares; if we build the walls, he labors to cast down the stones; if we serve God in sufferings and in conflicts — everywhere, Satan hinders us. He hinders our coming to Christ Jesus; he endeavors to hinder the completeness of our personal character.

Yet I am not alarmed that Satan hinders us, for it is a proof we are doing God's work — and in His strength, we shall win the victory and triumph over our adversary.[7]

Satan does not want the church to be fueled with a fearless passion and a desire to see God known and worshiped on every shore and among every tribe. He does all he can to keep the church consumed with its own building projects, its internal strife, and its entertainment. Remember who the real enemy is.

Finally, no matter what we endure for the sake of the gospel, we should always rejoice over their steadfast love of God:

Therefore, brothers, in all our distress and persecution we were encouraged about you because of your faith. For now we really live, since you are standing firm in the Lord. How can we thank God enough for you in return for all the joy we have in the presence of our God because of you? Night and day we pray most earnestly that we may see you again and supply what is lacking in your faith. (1 Thessalonians 3:7-10)

RESPONDING TO PERSECUTION THROUGH THE LENS OF COMMUNITY

We must not look down on those who are persecuted for their faith, for that would lead us to pride. We also must not put them up on a pedestal, for that would lead to idolatry. Instead, we need to look upon our persecuted brothers and sisters as family and a part of our community of faith. Hebrews 13:3 tells us, "Remember those in prison as if you were their fellow prisoners, and those who are mistreated as if you yourself were suffering." An early church mystic said, "We were created in the image of the laughter of the Trinity!" This means that we were created in the image of community: the Father, Son, and Holy Spirit. We must have community to fully know what a journey of faith in Christ is.

Of course, that community of faith begins in a local context, through a local church. But we must also come to know community in a historical context—to understand how and why we exist as the church today by reading about men and women who lived and served before us. Finally, we must have global perspective on community. We have the privilege to be in community with our brothers and sisters around the world.

If we want to understand the ways of God, discern the words of Jesus, and unlock the mysteries of the kingdom, then we must be in community with those persecuted in other lands. We must be in community with those who suffer degrees of injustice that we have never known on American soil.

A FEW PRACTICAL SUGGESTIONS ON HOW TO RESPOND

Because many in the world suffer for their faith and ministry in Christ, we must care. Here are a few suggestions for living out that compassion in practical ways:

Get informed on where persecution exists in the world. Subscribe to e-mail lists, purchase books, or talk to your missionary friends to educate yourself about where persecution is greatest today. Here are a few good places to start:

• Christian Freedom International (www.christianfreedom.org)

- Human Rights Watch (www.hrw.org)
- Amnesty International (www.amnesty.org)
- Christian Solidarity Worldwide (www.cswusa.com)
- The Voice of the Martyrs International (www.persecution.net)
- Open Doors (www.opendoorsusa.org)

Write your political leaders, both state and national, and inform them of your concern for the countries that persecute Christians. You can contact your federal representative and senator via e-mail by going to www.house.gov and www.senate.gov. In a similar way, you can contact your state officials by visiting your state's official website (www.[your state].gov).

Pray for those who are persecuted. Pray that Jesus will appear before the persecutors as He did to Saul on the road to Damascus. Prayer is vital and a great way to organize your small group or your whole church to support those who are being persecuted for their faith in Jesus Christ.

FOR REFLECTION AND DISCUSSION

1. Think back to a time in your life when you experienced a season of suffering. What did you learn from that experience? Did it bring you closer to God? Why or why not?
2. Which paradox of the gospel is the most difficult for you to understand? What could you do to understand it better?
3. Think back to a time you heard a story of someone being persecuted for his or her faith. How did it affect you?
4. Do you agree with the idea that people must die for Jesus Christ in various regions of the world in order for the church to grow? Why or why not?
5. Which Scriptures in this chapter spoke to you the most? How did they impact you?

chapter eight

A GOD OF JUSTICE

Injustice anywhere is a threat to justice everywhere.
DR. MARTIN LUTHER KING

Speak up for those who cannot speak for themselves,
for the rights of all who are destitute.
Speak up and judge fairly;
defend the rights of the poor and needy.
PROVERBS 31:8-9

Nuraj and Ramesh were normal Indian boys who were extremely poor and lived in a rural village. Their home was like most in their small village: made of mud and grass. One day, their world came crashing in on them when their father died. Worse, they were subsequently abandoned by their mother. The boys, ages five and seven, were sold by distant relatives to the local landlord because of a debt they had.

No longer would Nuraj and Ramesh spend their days attending school and playing with other children on the playground. Suddenly their days became exhausting, tedious, and miserably hot. The boys sat on stones for twelve hours each day and broke rocks into small pieces. They did this seven days a week, never getting a day to rest or enough to eat.

Nuraj and Ramesh

Thousands of children in India are in some sort of bonded labor like Nuraj and Ramesh. But unlike that of most of their peers, these boys' story has a happy ending. A pastor in their village heard of the boys and was determined to get them freed and cared for in an appropriate way. Through the pastor's efforts, the boys were released and brought to ServLife's ministry center in India in 1997. Thus, an orphanage was established.

When you read the story of these brothers, are there not emotions that stir within you? Do you not say to yourself, *How can anyone think of doing something like this to children?*

Well, the reality is that what happened to these boys goes on every day all around the world, effectively destroying the lives and hopes of thousands upon thousands of innocent children. It is unjust and wrong.

ANALYSIS LEADS TO PARALYSIS

In traveling through the world and ministering in different places, I have repeatedly found there is a cold apathy among many Christians when it comes to issues of injustice around the world. There is concern, but often that concern leads nowhere. Analytical thinking often leaves people feeling helpless and paralyzed. This is exactly what the Devil wants: unresponsive and inert Christians. We see the injustice on television. We read in missionary newsletters or hear reports at our church and are overwhelmed at the reality of wrong being done to the innocent. "What could I possibly do to help?" you may ask. Or you may also say to yourself, *There is just too much suffering. Nothing I did would make a real difference.*

However, if we are honest, deep inside our hearts something wells up and wants to take action. But often we do not know what to do.

Gary Haugen, founder of the International Justice Mission, says that when Christians are confronted with the injustices of the world, it is as if our hearts become like deer frozen in headlights of a car. The information that should provoke us to action does the exact opposite. The effect is similar to what happens when you eat a meal that is supposed to provide energy for your body but instead makes you feel like lying down and taking a nap.[1]

Solomon wrote,

> *Again I looked and saw all the oppression that was taking place under the sun:*
>> *I saw the tears of the oppressed —*
>> *and they have no comforter;*
>> *power was on the side of their oppressors —*
>> *and they have no comforter. (Ecclesiastes 4:1)*

Indeed, Solomon's reaction rings true for anyone who gazes out into a troubled world filled with so much pain, injustice, and human suffering. What can we do? Perhaps we cannot change the whole world at all once, but we can change the world one life at a time through the power of Christ.

In my view, there are three primary reasons why we should respond to issues of injustice around the world:

Because we know God. Eternal life is knowing God now — it isn't merely going to heaven when we die. Jesus said, "Now this is eternal life: that they may know you, the only true God, and Jesus Christ, whom you have sent" (John 17:3). As we come to know the God of the Bible, we clearly see His heart and passion for justice throughout His Word.

One of the common problems for many of us who follow Jesus Christ is that we are not often reminded of the Scriptures that speak on the theme of justice. Yet the Scriptures are filled with that theme. The Bible says, "The LORD loves righteousness and justice; the earth is full of his unfailing love" (Psalm 33:5). God said to Jeremiah,

> *"But let him who boasts boast about this:*
> *that he understands and knows me,*
> *that I am the LORD, who exercises kindness,*
> *justice and righteousness on earth,*
> *for in these I delight." (Jeremiah 9:24)*

God said to Isaiah,

> *"For I, the LORD, love justice;*
> *I hate robbery and iniquity.*
> *In my faithfulness I will reward them*
> *and make an everlasting covenant with them." (Isaiah 61:8)*

The Bible even tells us specifically what it means to seek justice:

> *"Learn to do right!*
> *Seek justice,*
> * encourage the oppressed.*
> *Defend the cause of the fatherless,*
> * plead the case of the widow." (Isaiah 1:17)*

In responding to issues of injustice, we must not merely observe but act. Jesus modeled equality and empowerment for the voiceless. Remember the woman at the well (see John 4) and the little children who sat on His lap (see Mark 10:13-16)? In both of these stories, Jesus modeled going against the religious viewpoint of the day. In Jesus' day, it was far out of the social norm for Jewish men to talk to a Samaritan woman or to interact with children in the street. These very acts communicated that we are all equal before God and should be treated justly.

God clearly tells us what our response to injustice should be. The Bible says,

> *"He has showed you, O man, what is good.*
> * And what does the LORD require of you?*
> *To act justly and to love mercy*
> * and to walk humbly with your God." (Micah 6:8)*

Because we are citizens of the kingdom of God. Why is so much of the church silent on the issue of injustice? Perhaps it is because of the way we preach the gospel of Jesus Christ. Much of the church emphasizes that salvation is mostly about "getting into heaven" and the implications here on earth are secondary. But the power of the gospel of Jesus Christ is not limited to our "eternal destiny"—it impacts every aspect of our lives in the here and now.

A primary theme in Jesus' teachings was the "kingdom of God." His parables were mostly insight and instruction about kingdom life. He said that the kingdom is not out there somewhere but is inside you (see Luke 17:21). He also prayed, "Your kingdom come, your will be done on earth as it is in heaven" (Matthew 6:10).

In God's kingdom, there will be no injustice; therefore, we should strive as Christians on this side of heaven to see justice exercised on the earth. Most would agree as well that the basic idea of God's kingdom is the reign and rule of God. When justice is achieved for the fatherless, the oppressed, the widow, and the poor in the name of Christ, God's kingdom is present, and God Himself is honored and glorified.

Because we are agents of hope in a world of sin. In Genesis 3, Adam and Eve chose to sin, and the aftermath is what came to be known as the Fall. Ever since that day, people in our world have been born into sin and are separated from God. We now live in a world where the wickedness of people's hearts leads them to commit incomprehensible acts. As a result, billions of people face poverty and millions of others are held as victims of people's greed, lust, power, and desire for control.

Yet in the midst of the evil that pervades our world, there is also the body of Christ. We are here to offer our hands as Jesus did when He was on the earth to touch people with acts of kindness and compassion. We as the church are the feet of Jesus to walk where people are hurting and to offer them the hope that is in God. We are the ears of Jesus to listen to those who suffer and to be a friend to them. We are the eyes of Jesus, always looking for the despised and rejected, that we might go and encourage them.

It has been said that the church of Jesus Christ is the sole hope of the world. I would argue that it is not the church but Jesus Christ Himself and His kingdom that is the hope for the world—and it is He and His kingdom that we are called to proclaim. A person can live forty days without food, four days without water, and four minutes without air, but no one can live even four seconds without hope. Hope is a powerful reality for everyone who breathes on this earth. No matter what culture you live in, the desperate need for hope is common to all.

We experience different degrees of hope throughout our lives. For example, there are plenty of "everyday hopes" we all share, such as the hope of finding a good place to park at the airport or the hope of not catching the flu. We also hold bigger hopes for our children to grow up healthy and succeed. And we have even bigger hopes that our lives will actually have meaning and make a difference in the world. In many of the cultures I have visited, people's hopes and dreams have been crushed because of economic or other forms of injustice. However, I have also witnessed many people in these oppressed regions of the world who possess an astounding, contagious hope—a hope that stems directly from their faith in Jesus Christ. As the Bible says, "we have this hope as an anchor for the soul, firm and secure" (Hebrews 6:19).

The South African missiologist David Bosch wrote that "Christian hope is both possession and yearning, repose and activity, arrival and being on the way. Since God's victory is certain, believers can work both patiently and enthusiastically, blending careful planning with urgent obedience, motivated by the patient impatience of the Christian hope."[2]

I am thrilled, as many are, to see so many Christians respond to Bono, the lead singer of the famous rock group U2, as he speaks out on HIV/AIDS issues in Africa, eliminating the debt of poorer nations, and other issues of injustice. But at the same time, I am saddened that Christians are not equally moved simply by reading God's Word—seeing His heart for the oppressed and hearing His cry against injustice throughout Scripture. God must look down on events in the world today and be saddened that His church is not doing all we can. These issues are not exclusively Bono's issues, after all. They belong to all of us. I believe great opportunities for the gospel of Jesus Christ will be available if we as the church move to action in combating human trafficking, bonded labor, the environment, HIV/AIDS, and other issues of justice.

HUMAN TRAFFICKING

Gune is the most beautiful little girl you could ever see. She is ten years old and has the face of an angel. But whatever physical attributes she's been blessed with have not shielded her from life's hardships. She lived with her poor, uneducated parents in a small village in rural Nepal. Her father consumed copious amounts of locally brewed alcohol almost every day and took out his misery on Gune and her mother.

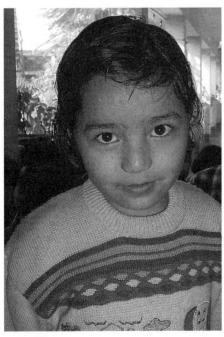

Gune

"The Hindu gods must be punishing me," he would often say to his family or to himself. "There is no hope."

After enduring one especially brutal night of drunkenness and violence, Gune's mother took a knife and killed her husband. Gune, who was seven years old at the time, watched in horror as the entire macabre scene played out before her eyes. The authorities arrested Gune's mother and threw her into jail, where she remains to this day. A local pastor heard about this story and brought Gune to ServLife Children's Home in India, where she now lives. At the children's home, she is given an education, meals, and, most importantly, love. Gune often tells me that she wants to be a doctor when she grows up, so she can help others just as she has been helped. She has also come to love Jesus.

"My favorite part of the movie of Jesus is when they hung Him on the cross because He died for my sins," she explains.

Every time I am with Gune, my heart is moved because I think of the life that could have so easily been hers: that of an enslaved prostitute, sleeping with fifteen to twenty men a day at a brothel in a big city in India. You see, young girls like Gune very often end up being trafficked into the extensive sex trade industry based in that region of the world. God's Spirit must compel us to come to the aid of all of these girls who suffer as innocent victims in this depraved industry.

Trafficking human beings is not the same as smuggling them. Human trafficking involves deceiving or coercing someone to move — either within a country or abroad through legal or illegal channels — for the purpose of exploiting him or her. Smuggling, on the other hand, is assisting someone for a fee to cross a border illegally.[3] Human trafficking has become a nine-billion-dollar-a-year global industry and is becoming increasingly entrenched within large organized crime rings.[4]

Some may think that human trafficking is only an issue outside the western world. Think again. It is impacting America. The U.S. State Department estimates that between eighteen and twenty thousand people are trafficked into the U.S. every year.[5] Every year, the American government alone spends about fifty-five million dollars to combat this issue.[6]

Trafficking involves the buying and selling of humans, usually women or children, for economic gain via means of force or deception. In Nepal, where my family lived and served for a number of years, it is estimated that two hundred thousand Nepalese girls under the age of sixteen have been trafficked into India as prostitutes.[7] Another human rights organization estimates that an additional six to seven thousand Nepalese girls end up in Indian brothels every year.[8] According to one expert, at least half of the one hundred thousand girl prostitutes between the ages of ten and fourteen in Bombay are originally from Nepal and are kept in brothels against their will.[9]

These are girls just like Gune.

This is a horrible reality. Human trafficking affects people of all ages, but the impact on young girls is especially profound, especially since these children cannot speak up for themselves. I believe there are three important ways we can respond to this atrocious injustice:

Prevention. Perhaps the most effective way to stop the trafficking of the innocent is by preventing it from happening in the first place. This is, of course, much more easily said than done. Such prevention would require change on many levels of society: through educating families at the grassroots level, passing stricter laws to combat organized crime, and working with organizations to provide economic development in areas where trafficking is rampant.

Providing opportunities for economic development is particularly important. When people have the basic ability to provide for themselves and pay for their children's education, they will not be so easily enticed by these unsavory "alternative" means of support. One of the ways children are trafficked is when the children's parents are approached by so-called "businessmen" who promise that their children can earn good money in their factories making products. They promise the parents that the children will be well cared for and will be able to send money back to them. The uneducated parents agree and send the children to some distant location, thinking they are helping both their children and themselves. They do not realize that they are sending their children to be beaten and forced into prostitution or hard labor. These parents are typically illiterate and extremely poor.

Rescuing and Caring for Young Victims of Sexual Exploitation in Nepal

They are deceived by the apparent opportunity to give their children a marketable skill and create a better life for themselves.

Education is also very important and can go a long way in helping communities that may be prone to this sort of predation. This is where I believe God may be calling some of you who are reading this to step in and help. Perhaps you are exceptional in business and have entrepreneurial talents, yet you are struggling with what to do with your life. Why waste your skills on simply making stockholders happy? Give your life to the cause of preventing human trafficking. Right now all around the world, there is great need for people who have the skills to set up and launch "micro-businesses" in areas where human trafficking is rampant.

A micro-business in the developing world can be set up for a mere two hundred and fifty to five hundred dollars. Examples of micro-businesses include setting up a small kiosk to sell fruit and vegetables, purchasing several goats to start a goat farm, or making bags or other handicrafts. Micro-business loans to local residents can be given with little or no interest, but the return on investment is huge in terms of lives saved. When the loan is paid back, the money can be used again to help others get started. There are some large organizations and governments that are doing this in very effective ways. But there are also thousands of grassroots organizations, churches, and individuals that are making a difference by helping the poor start their own businesses. Our organization alone has helped two hundred Sudanese refugees, mostly poor widows, start these kinds of businesses.

Intervention. In many places in the world, certain groups focus exclusively on rescuing victims from slavery but do nothing to help those victims become productive members of society. For that reason, many times the victims return to their life of slavery, because that is all they know. Therefore, a follow-up plan for getting these victims into homes, ministries, and educational institutions is absolutely crucial.

Vinay John

A more intentional intervention is needed to see that these people are placed in a healthy environment where they can be educated and loved.

Vinay John never planned to be a hero. But when the ServLife missionary and church planter in India got stopped one Sunday after church by a grandmother of three small children, he was about to embark on an heroic rescue mission that would save lives — and change his own.

Seema and Rebecca, ten and eight years old, were destined for the same life of prostitution

that had enslaved their mother, the old woman told ⌐
grandson, Samuel, was in danger too. What was she t
    Vinay took action and was able to bring the children, u....
to the Arunoday-Black children's home run by ServLife in north India.
Their mother, who had conceived all three via her vocation, consented
to give them up in hopes they might find a life better than hers.

Vinay John was trained by ServLife in the one-year training
school for local church planters and native missionaries. He graduated in 2005 and returned to his hometown of Jamshedpur, India. He
and his wife, Megha, have two infant sons, both paralyzed. Currently,
five families attend his church, which began in his home. His family
resists the message, he says, especially his brothers. But Vinay declares,
"Despite resistance from my family, I long to serve the Lord and share
the gospel with my own people."

Thanks to this ServLife missionary, three more children have been
spared the anguish of homelessness and prostitution. Instead, they're
experiencing safety, love, and the hope of Christ.

Rehabilitation. In order to rehabilitate the children who fall
victim to trafficking, many more orphanages and children's homes
are desperately needed. It was the apostle James who said, "Religion
that God our Father accepts as pure and faultless is this: to look after
orphans and widows in their distress and to keep oneself from being
polluted by the world" (1:27).

Perhaps God is calling you to move to a place in the world where
trafficking is happening and start a children's home so you can share the
love of Jesus Christ with children who have come out of this situation.
What a worthy goal and ambition for one's life! (For more information
on how you can pursue this goal, e-mail me at info2@servlife.org.)

MODERN-DAY SLAVERY

Slavery is still alive and thriving in the world. According to the United Nations, the word *slavery* today applies to a variety of human rights violations. In addition to traditional slavery and the slave trade, these abuses include the sale of children, child prostitution, child pornography, the exploitation of child labor, the sexual mutilation of female children, the use of children in armed conflicts, debt bondage, the sale of human organs, the exploitation of adult prostitution, and certain practices under apartheid.[10]

Here are a few examples of modern-day slavery:

Bonded labor. This takes place when a family receives an advance payment (sometimes as little as fifteen dollars) to hand a child over to an employer. Sometimes they are tricked into doing this. In most cases, the child cannot work off the debt, nor can the family raise enough money to buy the child back. The workplace is often structured so that "expenses" or "interest" are deducted from a child's earnings in such amounts that it is almost impossible for a child to repay the debt. "In some cases," according to the Human Rights Watch organization, "the labor is generational—that is, a child's grandfather or great-grandfather was promised to an employer many years earlier, with the understanding that each generation would provide the employer with a new worker, often with no pay at all."[11]

Bonded labor impacts at least twenty million people around the world. To repay the debt, they are forced to work long hours, seven days a week, every week of the year. They receive basic food and shelter as "payment" for their work but may never pay off the loan. These children, who are typically between seven and ten years of age, work twelve to fourteen hours a day and are paid very little or nothing.[12]

Child labor. This refers to children being made to work in exploitative or dangerous conditions. Tens of millions of children around the world work full-time. Child labor, often hard and hazardous, damages health for life, deprives children of education, and robs them of the normal enjoyment of their early years. Child labor is in great demand because it is cheap and because children are naturally easier to discipline than adults and usually too frightened to complain. Their small stature and nimble fingers are seen as assets by unscrupulous employers for certain kinds of work. It often happens that children are given jobs, when their parents are sitting at home, unemployed.

Early and forced marriage. This affects women and girls who are married without choice and are forced into lives of servitude, often accompanied by physical violence. Early and forced marriage happens on a regular basis among the poor around the world. Within nations throughout Africa, usually the boy pays a dowry to the woman's family in order to secure a bride. In India, it is the opposite: The girl's family has to pay a dowry to the boy's family. Many times in villages, young girls are given in marriage before they even reach puberty.

THE ENVIRONMENT

The psalmist wrote, "The earth is the LORD's, and everything in it, the world, and all who live in it" (Psalm 24:1). And the apostle John said, "Through him all things were made; without him nothing was made that has been made" (John 1:3). Clearly, the earth was created by God and belongs to Him. He causes all things to grow on the earth and has given food for humankind. What makes us think that the earth is our property as human beings? We are merely stewards and have a responsibility to care for what God has given us. One Bible scholar writes, "Because God made the earth and its fullness, all animals, plants, and vegetables, there can be nothing in it or them impure or unholy; because all are the creatures of God."[13]

Many Christians do think much about the environment and our stewardship of it as God's children. Yet we have a responsibility to care for all that God has created. However, if you look at our world today, you will see a planet in danger of becoming something far from what God originally created. We as followers of Christ must be concerned. Problems related to fresh water alone kill thousands of people every day. Pollution causes health issues that are damaging for life. Did you know that half of the forests that originally covered 46 percent of the earth's land surface are gone? Research shows that "only one-fifth of the earth's original forests remain pristine and undisturbed."[14]

Between 10 and 20 percent of all species face extinction in the next twenty to fifty years. Based on current trends, an estimated 34,000 plant and 5,200 animal species—including one in eight of the world's bird species—very well may become extinct. Almost a quarter of the world's mammal species will face extinction within thirty years. Up to 47 percent of the world's plant species are at risk of extinction. Sixty percent of the world's coral reefs, which contain up to 25 percent of all marine species, could be lost in the next two to four decades.

Hundreds of thousands of sea turtles and marine mammals are killed by irresponsible fishing practices every year. More than 20 percent of the world's known ten thousand freshwater fish species have become extinct, been threatened, or become endangered in recent decades. Sixty percent of the world's important fish stocks are threatened from overfishing. Desertification and land degradation threaten nearly one-quarter of the land surface of the globe. Over 250 million people are directly affected by desertification, and one billion people are at risk. The grassroots organization World Revolution states, "Global warming is expected to increase the earth's temperature by 3 degrees Centigrade (5.4 degrees Fahrenheit) in the next hundred years, resulting in multiple adverse effects on the environment, including widespread species loss, ecosystem damage, flooding of populated human settlements, and increased natural disasters."[15]

As we understand that God has placed us as stewards of the earth, we should care for it and respond to the problems facing the planet. Here are some practical suggestions for how you can start helping now:

ServLife's School in North India

- Recycle in your home, workplace, and church.
- Start a cell phone drive. Two hundred and fifty million used mobile phones are lying around in this country in landfills. Start a cell phone drive and collect old phones. Our mission has done this and has raised over $1,500 for our work around the world.
- Carpool, and drive less.
- Make a donation to drill clean-water wells in the poor regions of the world. This can be done for just a few hundred dollars. Thousands still die every day from contaminated water.
- Become more informed by becoming acquainted with the excellent organization Evangelicals for Social Action (www. esa-online.org).

LACK OF EDUCATION

There is an Indian proverb that says, "Educating your daughter is like watering your neighbor's garden." In India, as in many places in the world, the value of educating a girl is not very high. Today, a child in Mozambique can expect to go to school for two or three years, with luck. Meanwhile, a five-year-old European or North American child can expect to spend fourteen years in formal education.[16]

Today, nearly two decades after the rallying cry of "Education for All," there are still 125 million children in the world who never attend school. An additional 150 million children of primary age start school but drop out before they can read or write. Today, sub-Saharan Africa accounts for one-third of the total out-of-school population. If current trends continue, that region will account for three-quarters of the total by the year 2015. One in four adults in the developing world—872 million people—is illiterate, and the numbers are growing.[17]

Perhaps you are now realizing the importance of this issue and are wondering how you can help. Here is where to start:

- Give up your vacation time; instead, volunteer to teach in a region of the world where teachers are desperately needed.
- Sponsor a child's education. There are many trustworthy child-sponsorship organizations from which to choose.
- Collect used books and send them to schools around the world.
- Give up a year or two and go teach in the world.
- Tutor children who are at risk or volunteer in an after-school program in your area.

ACCESS TO MEDICINES

Oxfam International is a confederation of twelve organizations working together with over three thousand partners in more than a hundred countries to find lasting solutions to poverty, suffering, and injustice. Oxfam points out that when patented medicines are priced out of reach for poor patients—and out of reach for their governments, many of which can't afford to spend more than a few dollars per person per year on healthcare—people suffer or die needlessly.

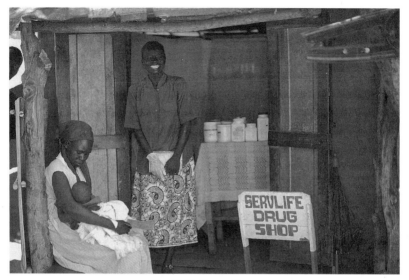

ServLife Drug Shop

As one international worker asks,

> It's a matter of values: Does the right of a corporation to earn a profit on its new product count more than the lives of millions of people? Shouldn't the balance between innovators' interests and the community's interest be protected somehow from such inaccessible pricing?
>
> In many poor countries, few people have health insurance, and spending on drugs comprises 50 to 90 percent of household costs for health care. In Burkina Faso, one of the poorest countries in west Africa, drugs account for more than 80 percent of the spending on health each year. Annual government spending on health care in many low-income countries is usually five to seven dollars per person. In many wealthy countries, it is sixteen hundred dollars.
>
> Consumers in rich countries spend more than $2.2 billion per year on the drug Claritin, used to treat the symptoms of hay fever. That is more than the total annual expenditure on drugs in all of sub-Saharan Africa.[18]

Though providing access to needed medicines is a huge problem worldwide, there is actually at least one easy way you can help. Older medicines or outdated or old medical supplies and equipment in America are all frequently discarded because there is no viable means to get them to charities that need them. There is always a need for people who can act as "brokers" between the U.S. medical industry and a host of service organizations who take these medicines and supplies from America to people around the world who need them. Here are three good groups to look to as a place to start:

- Project CURE (www.projectcure.org)
- Medical Assistance Program (www.map.org)
- FAME (www.fameworld.org)

ACCESS TO CLEAN WATER

Every day, people drink water from their sink. Some prefer to filter it or buy bottled water. But for more than one billion people on our planet, access to clean water is only a dream. Study after study has shown that whenever a community improves its water supply, hygiene, sanitation, and health improves dramatically. For example, the occurrence of diarrhea (a killer in many parts of the world) can be reduced by as much as 26 percent when basic water, hygiene, and sanitation are supplied to a village. Despite this fact, the current statistics tell a terrible story. Forty percent of the world's six billion people have no acceptable means of sanitation, and more than one billion people draw their water from unsafe sources.[19]

The World Health Organization says diarrhea-related diseases remain a leading cause of illness and death in the developing world. Every year about 2.2 million people die from diarrhea. Ninety percent of these deaths are among children, mostly in developing countries. A significant number of deaths are due to a single type of bacteria,

Water Is Not Easily Accessible in Many Places

shigella, which causes dysentery or bloody diarrhea. It is readily controlled by improving hygiene, water supply, and sanitation. Although no vaccine exists and antibiotics may be inaccessible to many people, an effective prevention is available. The simple act of washing hands with soap and water reduces shigella and other types of diarrhea by up to 35 percent.[20]

ECONOMIC INJUSTICE

According to the World Bank, half the world's people live on less than two dollars a day. Over one billion of those live on less than a dollar per day.[21] The assets of the two hundred richest people in 1998 were more than the total annual income of 41 percent of the world's people.[22] The World Development Movement reports, "Three families—Bill Gates, the Sultan of Brunei, and the Walton family—have a combined wealth of some $135 billion. Their combined value equals the annual income of six hundred million people living in the world's poorest countries."[23]

What's more, the richest one-fifth of the world

- consumes 45 percent of all meat and fish, while the poorest fifth consumes 5 percent;
- consumes 58 percent of total energy, while the poorest fifth consumes less than 4 percent;
- has 74 percent of all telephone lines, while the poorest fifth has 1.5 percent;
- consumes 84 percent of all paper, while the poorest fifth consumes only 1.1 percent;
- owns 87 percent of the world's vehicles, while the poorest fifth owns less than 1 percent.[24]

The "share" of the total global income among the poorest 20 percent of the world's people now stands at a miserable 1.1 percent, down from 1.4 percent in 1991 and 2.3 percent in 1960. It continues to shrink. On the other end of the spectrum, the ratio of the income of the top 20 percent to that of the poorest 20 percent rose from 30 to 1 in 1960 to a startling new high of 78 to 1 in 1994.[25]

Here is another way to put it that may make the situation clearer. If we could shrink the earth's population to a village of precisely one hundred people, with all the existing human ratios remaining the same, it would look something like this:

- There would be fifty-seven Asians, twenty-one Europeans, fourteen Americans (including North and South), and eight Africans.
- Fifty-two would be female; forty-eight would be male.
- Seventy would be non-white.
- Seventy would be non-Christian.

- Six individuals would possess 59 percent of the existing wealth, and all six of them would be from the United States.
- Eighty would live in substandard housing.
- Seventy would be unable to read.
- Fifty would suffer from malnutrition.
- Only one would have a college degree.
- Only one would own a computer.

I share these facts not to overwhelm you but because we as followers of Jesus must be educated. This information just scratches the surface, but I hope it will impress upon you the severity of issues around the world that demand our concern, attention, and response. I believe we act upon what we know and understand. I realize that sharing statistics like these can have the tendency to make us feel paralyzed and overwhelmed. This is where the Holy Spirit must inspire and empower our minds and hearts to receive this information and then grant wisdom on how we can respond effectively.

INJUSTICE AMONG ETHNIC GROUPS

So far I've focused on issues that impact billions of people on our planet. But there are also important issues of injustice and oppression that target specific ethnic groups across the globe. Many ethnic groups—from all religions—face oppression and severe injustice on a daily basis. We as Christians should speak out against such ethnic oppression, even when the victims are not Christian. Here are brief descriptions of just some of the ethnic groups facing oppression today. Many times these groups have few Christians among them. There can be great opportunity for empowerment and ministry when we speak out on their behalf, advocate for their cause, and serve them in the name of Jesus Christ.

The Saharawi people. In the northwest corner of the Sahara Desert live eight indigenous tribes collectively referred to as the

Saharawi. They are a people who have suffered incredible injustice and hardship. Centuries ago, they lived seminomadic lives in the Sahara and the coastal areas of what is now Western Sahara, formerly the Spanish Sahara, the last African colony. When Spain decolonized Western Sahara in 1975 at the urging of the United Nations, Morocco invaded, engaging in genocide and occupying the Saharawi land and homes. Thousands of Saharawi fled on foot across the Sahara. They found refuge across the Algerian border, where they set up four refugee camps with the help of the United Nations. Over 165,000 Saharawi have lived in these refugee camps for more than twenty-seven years, completely dependent on outside aid for food, shelter, and water. Despite the extremes of the Sahara, where temperatures soar over 135 degrees in the summer and drop to below freezing in the winter, the Saharawi have survived. They have formed a nation-in-exile that is recognized by nearly seventy nations. In 1965, the United Nations General Assembly called for the independence of the Western Sahara. In 1966, the International Court of Justice ruled that the Saharawi have the right to self-determination. The Saharawi and Moroccans agreed to a UN-negotiated ceasefire in 1991 to allow for a referendum to determine the will of the Saharawi people. This referendum has been repeatedly delayed by Morocco and has still not taken place.[26]

It is an amazing story of a beautiful people. I visited there a few years ago and was touched deeply by the sincerity and genuineness of these people. To further educate yourself on the struggle of the Saharawi, or to get involved, visit www.homelandonline.org.

The Tibetan people. In 1949, China began to put pressure on Tibet, declaring that it was not an independent nation but an "estranged" part of "motherland China." From the late 1940s through the 1950s, Mao Tse-tung employed the Chinese military in a gradual "squeeze play," which has culminated in the loss of Tibetan national sovereignty, the extermination of at least a million lives, and the displacement of hundreds of thousands. Tibetan culture has been all but wiped out. In addition, China has put crippling restrictions on religious practice inside Tibet and has implemented an educational system that has virtually rewritten Tibetan history from the perspective of the Chinese Communist Party. As a result of the Chinese government's systematic destruction of Tibetan religious life, of the six thousand monasteries that once thrived in Tibet, only thirteen remain today.[27]

In 1959, the spiritual and political leader of Tibet, the fourteenth Dalai Lama, was forced to flee Lhasa (the capital of Tibet) during an uprising in which thousands of Tibetans were massacred. He traveled over the Himalayas, eventually arriving at the Indian border. The Indian government received him with open arms, eventually providing him with a home in exile in the hills above Dharamsala, in the village of McLeod Ganj. This began a close relationship between India and the people of Tibet. Hundreds of thousands of refugees have followed the Dalai Lama's footsteps across the snowcapped Himalayas during the last five decades. Today there are still an average of fifteen hundred refugees making the journey to India and Nepal each year. Tibetans have endured unspeakable horrors, and what most of the world does not realize is that their story of persecution is not just a part of history—it continues to this day. The steady stream of refugees leaving Tibet for Nepal and India includes former political prisoners who have been beaten, raped, and abused for years because of their cries for freedom and dignity in the face of an oppressive regime.

The Dalits of India. In India there are approximately 250 million Dalits or "untouchables." This means that 25 percent of the population in India is Dalit. It also means that in a country where everybody is supposed to have equal rights and opportunities, one out of every four people is condemned as untouchable.

This tragedy is a direct consequence of India's caste system, which has remained entrenched in Indian culture for thousands of years. At the top are the Brahmans, the priests and arbiters of what is right and wrong in matters of religion and society. Next come the Kshatriyas,

A Dalit Girl in North India

who are soldiers and administrators. The Vaishyas are the artisan and commercial class, and finally, the Shudras are the farmers and the peasant class. These four castes are said to have come from Brahma's mouth (Brahman), arms (Kshatriyas), thighs (Vaishyas), and feet (Shudras). Beneath the four main castes is a fifth group, the Scheduled Caste. They literally have no caste. They are the untouchables, the Dalits, which means oppressed, downtrodden, and exploited social group. A Dalit is not considered to be part of human society but is instead something beneath it. Dalits are seen as "polluting" to higher caste people. If a higher caste Hindu is touched by an untouchable or even has a Dalit's shadow cross them, they consider themselves to be polluted and have to go through a rigorous series of rituals to be cleansed.

The Dalits perform the most menial and degrading jobs. They are typically poor, deprived, and socially backward. They do not have access to enough food, health care, housing, or clothing. They do not have equal access to education and employment. And they face considerable injustice in everyday life. Officially everybody in India has the same rights and opportunities, but the reality is quite different. The Dalits are the poorest of the poor in the world, and their caste status effectively strips them of their humanity. Dalits are denied access to public wells and public parks, and many restaurants use separate drinking glasses for Dalits. The ruling caste tells them they are Hindu, yet they are denied access to the temples, cannot become temple priests, and, due to lack of education, cannot even read their scriptures. Their women are often sold into bonded prostitution. Even finding a place to bury their dead is a problem. Seventy percent of Dalits live below the poverty line.

On November 4, 2001, thousands of Dalits traveled to New Delhi from all over India to denounce the oppressive system they have been living under. Even though the government tried to block the ceremony, a mass of people representing Dalits openly declared that they were leaving Hinduism for religions that allowed them freedom and gave them equality. Since then, Dalits have regularly identified themselves with other faiths. Many states in India are passing or trying to pass local laws that prohibit the Dalits from converting to other religions.

The Dalits are crying out for holistic reformation. Individuals and organizations from all over India are rising to the great need of the Dalits. But it will take the effort of people from all over the world partnering with those in India to see this movement have a sustaining effect on the fabric of Indian society. Since the majority of Dalits are illiterate, education is central to any program. The vast majority of secondary schools in India are English. In order for the Dalits to gain acceptance to these schools and to be able to function in the marketplace, they need English to be taught in primary schools. Beyond schooling, the Dalits need basic medical care, micro-loans for business development, and people who will show them love and concern.

❧ — ❧

When responding to an ethnic group or nation that has faced oppression and injustice, perhaps the place to start is to ask for forgiveness on behalf of former "westerners" who contributed to the problems or showed a lack of concern rather than acted as agents of positive change. This is especially helpful to remember if you find yourself talking to someone from a certain nation or ethnic group that has faced oppression and injustice. In fact, it is difficult to find an oppressed people group to whom this approach does not apply.

For instance, in any Muslim region, there is still deep animosity toward western influence and government policy. This concern is based on hundreds of years of history, in which many who claimed to be Christian did horrible things in the name of religion. Beginning in the eleventh century and continuing through the thirteenth century, Christians launched a series of armed expeditions, or Crusades, throughout the Arab world. The West wanted to free the Holy Land from Islamic influence. Most all of the Muslim world recalls this history; it is embedded deep into their psyche.

Even today Muslim communities see oppression and injustice going on before their very eyes by those who they perceive as Christian. The ethnic cleansing that went on in Kosovo during the 1990s is an example of this. Do you ever wonder how the Muslim world views the events of that time? Ninety-five percent of all Albanians who were "ethnically cleansed" in Kosovo were Muslim. Who were their killers? Serbians, who are orthodox Christian by ethnic and cultural identity.

Religion has been used as a tool for oppression for centuries. As one scholar put it, "religion is not merely adherence to creeds or doctrines. Religion is the fundamental shaper of human life, social structures, and systems, sometimes positively so, sometimes not." We as Christ followers need to seek out opportunities to act as ambassadors of forgiveness toward the oppressed people of the world so that doors may be reopened for the gospel to be shared.

When Muslims think of a Christian, many of them throughout

the world do not know the difference in practice and belief between Slobodan Milosevic and Billy Graham. Milosevic, a Serbian Christian, was tried for genocide against Muslims. When ministering with or around Muslims, you should always remember this and sensitively yet boldly let them know that you do not agree with everything that Christians have done to Muslims throughout history. You will be amazed at their open response and the opportunity for trust and relationship that will come as a result. Many of us in the western Christian world think only about what certain people from the Muslim world have done to us in the West. However, let us not forget history and what we as the "Christian West" have done to Muslims.

Not only do the Crusades hinder our ability as Christians to impact certain people groups who are oppressed, but western colonization does as well. Before colonization ended in the mid-twentieth century, many regions of the world were governed and controlled by western governments, mostly European: the Dutch in Indonesia, the Spanish in the Philippines, the British throughout Africa and Asia, and the French in various parts of Africa. During the centuries of colonization, many of these European countries realized the importance of Christian missionaries to help set up education and commerce. We owe a great deal of debt and honor to these western missionaries who pioneered, suffered, and served in the nineteenth century.

However, most of them did not just bring the hope and love of the gospel of Christ; they brought along their culture as well, both the good and bad of it. Look at David Livingstone, the famous British missionary who served and explored Africa. During his missionary service, he believed he was not to stay in one place but to go on "God's Highway," as he called it. Livingstone wrote, "I must move on. I will bring Christianity, commerce, and civilization to the people of Africa."[28] I would add that he also brought his culture with him, as anyone does who moves to another culture. We never become 100 percent separate from our home culture when we move to another country. Many in the world despise the West today as a result of the impact those days of colonization had on their culture.

When I travel through India, especially the poorer and less educated areas, everyone just assumes I am British, simply because India was colonized by Britain for three hundred years. England did many good things during that time, such as establishing hospitals, creating the train system, improving education, and so on. However, with those benefits also came missionaries who were perceived by the Indians as determined to change the culture of India or to take resources from the local people for their own gain. It's critical that we understand these issues as we move out to minister and love individuals and entire ethnic groups in the world.

In addition to seeking understanding and asking forgiveness, we must also speak up on behalf of those who are being oppressed and do what we can to help them. When you speak out for different people groups who have faced injustice from other political regimes or governments, do not be afraid to speak your mind. But be sure you speak with great caution and wisdom. Remember Jesus' advice to his disciples in Matthew 10:16: "I am sending you out like sheep among wolves. Therefore be as shrewd as snakes and as innocent as doves."

Acts of injustice and oppression are usually rooted in political motivations—a desire to control money, land, or power in government. For that reason, we must use wisdom when speaking out in support of the oppressed, especially if we are living and ministering in a volatile area. I have seen far too many western workers jeopardize their ministry and even get thrown out of a country because they openly proclaimed their support for one political side or the other. Try to do your work of ministry "through the conflict" as opposed to speaking out in support of a certain side of the conflict. In other words, whatever direction the political process goes, use caution as you speak your mind, especially if you are living in that country. By taking political sides, you could potentially isolate yourself from those who need Christ but who do not share your viewpoint. We should strive to do the work of the kingdom no matter what is going on—in peace or war, famine or prosperity.

HOW CAN I RESCUE THEM?

Praxis comes from the Latin phrase "to be put into practice." We should always look at the praxis of the gospel in relationship to issues of justice or for other issues in the Christian life. What does the good news of Jesus Christ and His kingdom mean for me, my family, and my community? How can I put the gospel into action?

In many cases, I believe that social justice activists or mission mobilizers have become too pragmatic in their requests for help, providing only a short list of their own ideas on what we should do and how we should do it rather than simply explaining the full breadth of the need and allowing the Holy Spirit to direct people to act as they are inspired. The Holy Spirit is always wanting to breathe creativity into the church so that our original and fresh perspectives can be mobilized to provide a host of unique and potent agents for change, reconciliation, and healing throughout the world. I have tried to explain why we should act justly and love mercy as followers of Jesus, as well as give you some help in getting started. However, it is up to you to allow God to move on your heart and direct you in what He is specifically calling you to do. But whatever it is, start now!

- Start praying daily that God will give you wisdom, direction, and vision.
- Gather a community to meet regularly to pray together and discuss issues of justice and ways to get others involved and educated.
- Go to your pastor and other church leaders and share what

God is teaching you. Ask if you can lead a "justice group" within your church. Hopefully, your church will empower you and help you. If not, don't give up.

- Commit to praying daily for ministry workers who are responding to the issues of injustice in the world.
- Seek ways to raise money through an event, concert, or sports tournament for a ministry that helps the oppressed.

God works through people. He could have chosen to work through angels, but He chose to work through you and me: flawed and needy human beings. Through the ages, God has taken broken people and made them whole. He has taken abused people and healed them of their pain and allowed them to minister grace and love to others. God wants to do the same with you. Our God is a rescue God—He rescues us from our sin, death, and despair and gives us hope, meaning, and eternal life. God is in the business of taking people just like you and me and using us as conduits of hope and justice to the oppressed. We should not rely solely on the government to intervene. We should not look only to the "professional" minister or missionary to do the job. We are all participants with God in His mission throughout the world.

FOR REFLECTION AND DISCUSSION

1. Have you experienced a country where people did not have access to clean water or good medicines? How did this make you feel? What did it make you want to do?
2. Read Proverbs 3:27-28. When dealing with those who face injustice, what are some ways we can respond?
3. Can you remember the first time you really struggled with inequality in the world? What prompted the struggle? How might God have been speaking to you through that struggle?

4. Who could you ask to get together with on a weekly basis
   to pray and talk about issues described in this chapter? How
   could taking this simple step help bring positive change to
   the world?

chapter nine

THE STORMS THAT RAGE WITHIN

*Most of us arrive at a sense of self and vocation only after a
long journey through alien lands. But this journey bears no
resemblance to the trouble-free "travel packages" sold by the
tourism industry. It is more akin to the ancient tradition of
"pilgrimage"—a transformative journey to a sacred center
full of hardships, darkness, and peril.*

PARKER PALMER

The airport immigration officer looked at me with sadness in his eyes
and said, "I am so sorry."

My family and I were about to fly back into Thailand from Nepal
just two days after the worst natural disaster in the nation's history.
The massive tsunami hit Asia the day after Christmas 2004.

I wondered what the officer thought as he saw me approach with
my young son and pregnant wife. Normally the immigration line is
filled with people from all over the world coming to enjoy Thailand's
exotic beaches. However, this day was different.

Our family had been stuck away in a small hotel on the India-
Nepal border when the tsunami ravaged the shores of many nations
all over Asia. We watched on our little television set the horrific images
supplied by the BBC and CNN. We wondered if our two-room duplex

had been destroyed. Just three months before the tsunami hit, God had led us to establish a living and working space in southern Thailand as we developed ministry opportunities throughout Asia.

And at last, there we were, at the airport, trying to return to our Thai base. The immigration officer assumed we were just tourists, and that's when he said, "I am so sorry." What an insight into the Thai people—so warm, loving, and inviting.

"We live here," I replied. "We live here in a house."

He was shocked to see us return just a few days after most foreigners had left the area.

"You do not have to be sorry," I continued. "But *we* are very sorry that so many beautiful Thai children died and many adults also lost their lives in your wonderful country."

We were told that the return flight to Bangkok, one of just twelve that day, was completely packed. Our flight, which was supposed to be loaded with several hundred people, had only a few dozen. How true it is that most people hurry to escape chaos, pain, and destruction, while few hurry toward it to try to help. I began to wonder what we could really do. It seemed overwhelming, like trying to take a drink from a fire hose.

When we finally landed and left the airport in the evening, we took a short drive around Nai Yang beach, the beach close to our duplex that we went to often. Every store, restaurant, dive shop, and bar was gone. Elise and I looked at each other, wondering if our friends—the ones we talked and ate with, the ones who loved to hold our son—were dead or alive. Few words were spoken between us. We were both in shock.

The next day I contacted a few Thai friends and a Thai pastor and told them I wanted to go see the devastated fishing villages along the

Thai Christians Distribute Relief Items to Tsunami Survivors

coast. We set out early in the morning, only to be exposed to death, destruction, and despair unlike anything that nation or the world had ever seen. We drove two hours north and, mile after mile, saw cars that had been thrown into rice patty fields, buildings completely demolished, and rubble everywhere.

As we drove through one community that was completely destroyed, I glanced over to a pile of debris and saw a Winnie-the-Pooh stuffed animal lying next to a flattened house. Tears filled my eyes because "Pooh" was the first word my son had spoken when he'd begun to transition from baby-talk gibberish to real words.

I could not imagine the pain of losing a child to an act of nature. The horror and grief that would be carried through the rest of any parent's life was too much for me to comprehend. Who did this Winnie-the-Pooh toy belong to? A young Thai boy? A young Thai girl? Pain, horror, and death were everywhere.

SEARCHING FOR HOPE

The days, weeks, and months following the tsunami were filled with several windows of hope in the lives of the Thai people. However, I

The Destruction and Impact of the Tsunami in Thailand

know that many people's lives were broken, bruised, battered—and holding on by a very thin thread. Hope is often hard to find in the midst of crisis, but it is possible.

One day as we went out to the camps that housed survivors, we met a mother who did not eat or sleep for three days after the tsunami because she was looking for her two-year-old son's body. He was swept out of her arms by the rush of water. I sat in her newly constructed ten-by-ten-foot structure, built by the Thai government, while she offered me bottled mineral water as a token of her gratitude. Her eyes filled with tears as she asked to see a photo of my son, who was the same age as her own.

As our team began to think of ways we might provide help in the midst of the chaos, we approached a local Thai church and asked, "What do you plan to do?"

The pastor replied, "We have 7,800 baht and fifty books to distribute." (That is a little less than two hundred dollars.) I then began to imagine if we could give financial aid and allow the local Thai people to distribute it, talk with the survivors, and pray with them. That's what we began to do.

Our first grant to the churches was a mere five thousand dollars. With these funds, many goods were purchased that had not been provided by larger relief groups, which were working on larger infrastructure projects such as restoring power, bulldozing wreckage, and removing debris. We started with about ten churches in the region (all with average sizes of twenty to thirty members), and our outreach began to gain momentum. Soon more funds came in, and we enlisted the help of more churches, small as they were, to distribute numerous household items to people. Out of this demonstration of love in action, relationships were formed, comfort was provided, and meaningful conversations about Christ occurred.

More and more volunteers from America began coming to work with us. One day, a tsunami survivor greeted one of the volunteer workers with this question: "What is that around your neck? A cross?" The survivor later told how some children who were living next to him all wore that same symbol around their necks, even as the tsunami hit. None of them perished. He later said that all of his own children had died. He wanted to know the meaning and the power behind this symbol that saves.

Some time later, I met Kamolthip Sridaskoal, the owner of a tiny business that sells yogurt from the back of a motorbike. Meeting this woman filled me with much-needed hope. She had been a follower of Jesus Christ for about five years and had chosen to follow Christ before her husband did. The day the tsunami hit, her Buddhist neighbors invited Kamolthip to join them for lunch and singing. But just minutes before the waves struck her small fishing village, she received a phone call asking her to come bring her yogurt to sell some distance away. She immediately hung up and left her house on her motorbike. Shortly thereafter, the waves hit, but she escaped! The entire Buddhist family and everyone in their house died.

As I talked with Kamolthip, she told me this story, and tears filled her eyes.

"I guess God is keeping me alive so I can tell survivors about His great love," she said. "I don't know. I am confused why I am alive and others died, but I do know I want everyone to hear about Him."

Kamolthip is now serving as a leader of a new church in a district of fifty thousand people.

After meeting with Thai pastors, my teammates and I began to think about the long-term spiritual and physical care we might provide for these shell-shocked survivors. We started to search for a building to purchase to donate to a local church. In Thailand, especially southern Thailand, you do not see many churches—lots of Buddhist temples, but few churches.

As we looked at buildings for sale, we came across one that caught my eye. It was structurally sound, on a main road, centrally located between several communities, and very close to the major town in the district. Just one problem: There was a four-foot-high anthill that had grown as the building sat empty for several years. To westerners, that wouldn't seem too hard to solve—just bring in an exterminator or some explosives. But to a Thai person, an anthill is a sign that evil spirits live in the building. Therefore, no one would purchase or rent the place.

What a great opportunity, I thought. *We've got to get this place.*

It turned out that the building was formerly a Thai bar, which usually means a brothel. As we spoke with people in the community, they would always raise their eyebrows in surprise and wonder why

Helping in the Rebuilding Process in Southern Thailand

in the world we would want a former brothel inhabited by evil spirits. Then my pastor friend Sujit would say to them, "Greater is the Spirit of God in us than the evil spirits in the world or in that house!" The Thai people would always be fascinated, and the conversation would go on for another thirty minutes.

The building was purchased. We thoroughly cleaned, painted, and made it a place of beauty. Today, you can go there and see a small band of believers, many of whom became Christians after the tsunami. Furthermore, we launched a revolving loan program to help tsunami survivors start businesses. The *Bangkok Post* even had an article about these developments.

Through all of these experiences, one of the most wonderful things to see was the Thai counselors and psychologists talking to tsunami survivors, helping them to work through the grief and emotional trauma. The lifelong impact of pain, suffering, and hurt would be immense. Those thousands of people, whose lives were shattered and smashed by the tsunami, were also left to deal with the ravages of internal storms. After witnessing firsthand the mass destruction and overwhelming loss of life, I'm not sure how anyone could get through such a crisis without God's strength. Thank the Lord that He is available and eager to help us all through our darkest times.

STORMS HIT ALL OF US

If we are honest, we know that terrible storms don't just happen in faraway places and not just in the literal sense. Sometimes we are engulfed by heartaches and hardships that rock our emotional and spiritual lives. At times, there are vast sea swells that knock us over and prevent us from picking ourselves up and being the people God desires for us to be. Emotional pain is present in all of us to some degree, depending on the kinds of traumas we have experienced and the misfortune we have encountered. Perhaps it was a painful childhood or unwise choices that created the storms that now rage within. Perhaps it is the result of another person's actions toward us that has created this emotional tsunami.

The reality of storms in our lives is not a question of *if* they will happen but *when*. And when storms do come, we should seek to understand the source. This is not always easy and may require a professional counselor to serve as a guide through the process. Failing to get to the real issues is like replacing the "check engine" indicator on your car dashboard instead of addressing the actual problem causing the motor to malfunction. We are a society that wants quick fixes and instant solutions. We wear masks to fool people into thinking everything's okay, even when it's not.

The storms that rage within us can vary, but they are usually linked to our emotions. God created emotions, and they have their place. God Himself expresses passion, zeal, anger, and even jealousy (see Psalm 2:4-5; Zephaniah 3:17; Exodus 34:14). He is an emotional

God, and we are emotional beings, because we were created in His image. We were created to experience emotion in our journey with God. Injustice in the world should make us angry, meaningful relationships should bring us joy, and the death of someone close to us should cause us to mourn.

As we read the Gospels, we see Jesus expressing many different emotions, including His tenderness with children, His anger at the temple, and His grief over the death of Lazarus. Surely God desires His children to be emotionally healthy and whole people. In our desire to follow, serve, and please God, we should carefully attend to our emotional well-being and wholeness. I realize this is often easier said than done.

Once while I was living in Asia (long before the tsunami), I went swimming in the ocean and was knocked down by a huge wave. I got up, confident that I could balance myself and stand on my own two feet, when I was promptly flattened by another wave. Then, reeling and unsteady, I struggled to my feet once again, only to be bowled over by a *third* wave. What an image of life! We get up, only to find ourselves being knocked down again and again.

But as followers of Christ, we are imbued with the hope that we can overcome and prevail—and in so doing, we will experience emotional health and freedom in our journey. Though God never said our years on earth would be easy and comfortable, He did promise that we could have full and abundant lives through Him (see John 10:10).

I also believe there's another important aspect to this issue: The healthier and more stable we are, the more we will be able to minister effectively to others. The more we have attended to our own storms, the more we can help others through theirs. As we consider ways we might reach out to people in our communities and around the world, let's do all we can to equip ourselves—and allow God to equip us—by addressing personal, spiritual, and emotional issues that might hold us back.

With this in mind, let's briefly look at four emotional storms that many people face.

The Storm of guilt and shame. Shame exists when we see ourselves as fundamentally inadequate and flawed. Guilt is usually a result of our behavior. Shame can be related to guilt, but it has more to do with defining who we are at the core. In short, we feel guilt about *what we do*; we feel shame about *who we are*.

There is a purpose for these emotions: to let us know that we are sinners and have sinned. Most of us do not need convincing of this fact, but the truth is that we have all sinned and failed to reach God by our own efforts (see Romans 3:23). Shame is what Adam and Eve experienced after they sinned before God in Genesis 3.

The helpful kind of shame people experience leads them to the recognition that they are sinners in need of a savior. However, for some, shame does not go away when they turn to Christ. This is where shame becomes damaging and destructive for believers. Once shame has done its job—convinced us of our need for salvation in Christ—it should be buried along with all of our sins that God forgave. As Paul said, "therefore, there is no condemnation for those who are in Christ Jesus, because through Christ Jesus the law of the Spirit of life set me free from the law of sin and death" (Romans 8:1-2). When we experience shame, we must believe in Jesus Christ and receive His atoning work on the Cross.

But some people continue to struggle with shame. Often, a victim of abuse—whether sexual, emotional, or physical—will still experience shame and need ongoing counseling to be freed from it. When dealing with continuing and unjustified shame, we should not stay idle but take action. Reject the Devil's accusations and affirm who you are in Christ. Develop relationships with people who treat you as an image-bearer of God.

Guilt usually comes when we realize that we have broken God's moral law in thought, word, or deed. When we experience guilt, we need to identify the sin in our lives and confess it to God and someone else. There is power in confessing sin to our brothers and sisters in Christ. James said, "Confess your sins to each other and pray for each other so that you may be healed" (5:16). Though God is, of course, the one who forgives our sins, it's clear that speaking openly and honestly with other people fosters healing.

God created believers to be in community with one another—for encouragement, support, and mutual accountability. A trusted fellow believer can provide perspective on our wrongdoing, help think through some of the reasons behind it, and, most of all, help us steer clear of future offenses. It is always a good idea to confess our sin to someone of our own gender who will keep us accountable.

The Storm of anger. There is a difference between "an angry person" and "a person who gets angry." Some people cannot control their anger—in fact, they are controlled by it. Then there are those who can manage their anger (at least most of the time) and typically become angry for legitimate reasons.

There are many sources of anger. When we see prejudice and injustice, we *should* experience anger. God hates injustice. This is a proper kind of anger—it can motivate us to take action. Of course, sometimes our own sin and selfishness result in anger. We might think, *I can't have my way, and I'm mad about it.* That's the kind of anger that can only be unhealthy and unproductive.

For some of us, we have not had good role models to show us how to handle anger in a healthy way. We are busy and want to avoid conflict with people. Often pain from the past oozes out in anger. Some tend to fall into the trap of denying their anger, stuffing it inside, only to have it burst out later on. This requires healing, and healing is a process.

The point is that anger—wherever it comes from—will turn into bitterness if not resolved. Anger that is not dealt with has a way of growing more and more intense. Those "cloudbursts" of anger can evolve into a fierce storm.

The Storm of depression. We all get depressed sometimes, often due to circumstances or situations that weigh heavily on us. But some types of depression have far more severity and longevity than merely "feeling down" on occasion. Depression is not merely experienced by writers, painters, and musicians, although it is proven that the artistic temperament is more prone to melancholy. (Read the songwriter and poet's words in Psalm 13, 77, and 88.) Depression is also the most common issue in mission personnel, probably due to high stress, overwork, isolation, lack of support systems, and inaccessibility to professional counseling and other health resources.[1]

Depression is often camouflaged in a variety of symptoms and manifestations. Common symptoms include chronic fatigue, persistent insomnia, loss of appetite and weight, decreased energy, inability to concentrate, loss of pleasure in activities one usually enjoys, excessive and inappropriate guilt, and social withdrawal. Depression can show up as decreased work performance and social interaction, impatience and irritability, and even hostility.

It is usually suggested that if depression lingers longer than two weeks, you should seek professional help. Depression is often caused by a person's physiological makeup or chemical imbalance, and in such cases medication is often recommended.

The Storm of burnout. Burnout is to deplete oneself, exhaust one's physical, mental, emotional, and perhaps spiritual resources, and wear oneself out by excessive striving to meet unrealistic expectations imposed by oneself or others.

Richard Swenson, MD, has studied and written extensively on this topic. He says,

> *Burnout is that point where something within you breaks. It is that point where you quit trying, when you finally throw up your hands and say, "I don't care anymore. I don't care who sees me. I don't care who hears me. I don't care about anything. I just want out."* . . .

Burnout is common among the spiritually minded. They are often very sensitive and tormentingly conscientious. They see the pain, and then they internalize it. They want to help the wounded and rescue the world. But they don't always realize that they were not designed to carry the entire global burden on their individual backs.[2]

The causes of burnout can be numerous. When someone has the inability to admit their limitations, unrealistic expectations, or impossible standards, burnout is highly likely at some point. Also, grief that is not handled and processed properly greatly contributes to burnout. Grief does not always involve the death of a love one; it can also involve the loss of a dream, a vocation, family unity, or a relationship. It is vital that you experience the pain and share your feelings of loss with a trusted friend or counselor.

I believe it is critical for all of us to establish boundaries and identify limitations in our lives and ministries. As Dr. Swenson points out, many believers have unrealistic expectations for themselves and others, and we end up taking on more than is humanly possible to handle. Sometimes we need to say no to *good* opportunities so we can say yes to the *best* ones. One of the biggest lessons I've learned is that God will accomplish His plan with or without me. He is not dependent upon *me* to carry out His will and achieve His purposes. We are valued by God not on the basis of what we *do* for Him but on the basis of who He is and His relentless love for us.

God wants our lives to have balance, rhythm, and a reasonable pace. We often hear only how the Lord wants us to be good stewards of our money. Surely He wants us to also be wise stewards of our energy, rest, time, commitments, and emotional reserves. When we are, we will be able to go about His work with wholehearted enthusiasm and passion.

MOVING TOWARD EMOTIONAL HEALTH

We've discussed some of the common emotional storms people face. So how do we move toward health and wholeness? No matter the storms that rage within us, we can all learn a lot from the Old Testament story of Elijah. This prophet of the Lord became so overwhelmed by his duties and setbacks and the weight of his responsibilities that he became very depressed. Elijah went a day's journey into the desert. "He came to a broom tree, sat down under it and prayed that he might die. 'I have had enough, LORD,' he said. 'Take my life; I am no better than my ancestors'" (1 Kings 19:4).

I imagine most of us have uttered words similar to Elijah's at some point: "I've had it. I can't go on. This is too much."

After telling the Lord he'd "had enough," Elijah then "lay down under the tree and fell asleep" (verse 5).

I appreciate God's response to Elijah. He did *not* say, "C'mon, quit your whining and lollygagging. There's work to be done!" No, God sent an angel to provide sustenance and nourishment: "All at once an angel touched him and said, 'Get up and eat.' He looked around, and there by his head was a cake of bread baked over hot coals, and a jar of water. He ate and drank and then lay down again" (verses 5-6).

How great is that? God sent the depressed prophet hot bread right out of the oven and a pitcher of water—and then let him sleep some more. The angel came back a second time with another serving of food and drink. And then we read, "Strengthened by that food, [Elijah] traveled forty days and forty nights until he reached Horeb" (verse 8).

What a classic picture of a servant of God who became discouraged, dispirited, and dejected by the storms of life. And God met him right where he was. The Lord knows our human frailties and limitations. As God's people, sometimes we want to overspiritualize our issues, when the best thing to do is take care of ourselves with proper rest and nourishment.

The story of Elijah is a great lesson for those of us going through a difficult time or who know someone who is. We need to preserve our own strength and energy for the journey ahead, and we should encourage our brothers and sisters in the faith to do likewise.

If you're in the midst of a storm — or want to prepare for when the next one hits — keep in mind these steps for taking care of yourself:

Eat, sleep, and exercise. We are a nation of sleep-deprived people who eat the wrong foods and don't exercise enough. Basic things such as proper sleep, healthy eating habits, and a consistent exercise regimen go a long way toward keeping us strong — physically, emotionally, and spiritually.

What's more, God gave us the gift of "endorphine release." Euphoria combats depression and the effects of stress through a chemical release in our brain that makes us feel good. This is the "natural high" that distance runners talk about. But it isn't limited to people who run marathons. Other ways to activate a release of endorphins include laughing, petting an animal, receiving a massage, being exposed to the sun or other light sources, and listening to calming music. Researchers say that if you find yourself yawning on a consistent basis, the likelihood of a lack of endorphins is real.[3] When you are experiencing emotional hurt and pain, you may not feel like exercising or engaging in other activities that provide a God-given boost. But those are the times you need it most.

Restore your environment. God created beauty in the Garden of Eden, where man and woman first lived. In that place, there was rest, relaxation, enjoyment, and pleasure. In our fallen world, our senses are assaulted on a daily basis. We grow weary, overstimulated, and fatigued. Restoring emotional vitality may mean looking at ways to "recreate Eden" in your own home or work environment. Utilize music, art, fragrances, and lighting to enhance your living and work spaces. Look for ways to promote calm and serenity while diminishing chaos and clutter. This can be done without having to spend a great deal of money—it's often just a matter of creativity and organization.

Cultivate uplifting thoughts. Where you let your thoughts lead, your heart and soul will follow. Your thoughts have a powerful ability to lift your mood and attitude—or tear them down. Fill your mind with healthy, positive, optimistic thoughts. One of the key Scriptures on this subject comes from the apostle Paul: "Whatever is true, whatever is noble, whatever is right, whatever is pure, whatever is lovely, whatever is admirable—if anything is excellent or praiseworthy—think about such things" (Philippians 4:8). We should memorize Scripture, poetry, music lyrics that inspire, or love letters from our spouse to fill our minds with enriching thoughts.

Stay connected to others. As I mentioned earlier, God created us to be involved with one another, to be linked and joined with fellow believers. Jesus Himself had a close friend, John, the one whom He loved. He also had three people—Peter, James, and John—in His inner circle. Then He had all twelve of the disciples that He traveled with, ate with, and talked with. If Jesus saw the importance of being connected with others, so should we.

Seek professional help if needed. A generation or two ago, there was a stigma attached to seeking treatment from a psychologist or other mental-health professional. The message was, "You've got to have *serious* emotional problems to go see a psychologist." Thankfully, that kind of thinking has largely disappeared over the past few decades. Trained and qualified counselors offer tremendous help for a variety of issues. Do not let anyone tell you to just pray and read your Bible and your emotional problems will go away. Sure, God and His Word are our ultimate sources of healing. But I also believe that the Lord uses gifted therapists to facilitate and foster growth and wholeness.

Don't let emotional storms keep you from being and doing what God wants you to do. A cursory study of history will reveal some of the most effective leaders in both the church and society who struggled through numerous emotional storms. People such as Winston Churchill, George Washington, Abraham Lincoln, Søren Kiekergaard, Charles Spurgeon, and the famous missionary Adoriam Judson all struggled through storms and went on to achieve great things. Embrace your pain and do not run from it. God has promised to see you through whatever hardship you face—and He always keeps His promises.

FOR REFLECTION AND DISCUSSION

1. What "storms" have you experienced in your life? How did you get through those situations?
2. In this chapter, we looked at four common storms people face: shame and guilt, anger, depression, and burnout. What other storms experienced by many people would you add to this list?

3. Why is it important to work through our own emotional, physical, and spiritual storms even as we seek to help others through their own?

4. In what practical ways can you help people you know weather the storms in their lives?

5. How have you experienced God's power and provision to get through difficult times?

chapter ten

A DIFFERENT KIND OF POWER

*A Cherokee elder sitting with his grandchildren told them,
"In every life there is a terrible fight—a fight between two
wolves. One is evil: he is fear, anger, envy, greed, arrogance,
self-pity, resentment, and deceit. The other is good: joy,
serenity, humility, confidence, generosity, truth, gentleness,
and compassion." A child asked, "Grandfather, which wolf
will win?" The elder looked him in the eye. "The one you
feed."*

CHEROKEE PROVERB

The following is an entry from my blog. Titled "An Angelic Encounter," it appeared in early 2004:

I recently took a short trip down to India, where I believe God was hearing the prayers of His people and sent an angel to save me from danger. It was a moment that left me truly humbled and thankful before God. I flew to New Delhi, where I was to get on another flight to visit a ServLife missionary serving among Tibetan refugees living in the mountains in northern India. My flight ended up being canceled, so I took another plane. I flew to Kashmir and then hired a car to drive five more hours through three states to reach McLeod Ganj, where the Dalai Lama lives along with five thousand Tibetans in exile.

We had been driving for several hours, and it was dark outside, when my driver suddenly announced that he would take me no farther. After realizing I could not convince him otherwise, he dropped me off about forty miles short of my destination. I was forced to hop on the local public transportation, which in this case was a large four-door jeep.

About eight men were in the vehicle. As I climbed in, I detected a strong smell of alcohol. I immediately began to pray. Indeed, without knowing my situation, many of you were perhaps praying at this moment for me as well. After about twenty minutes of driving, we pulled off the main road and got on a dirt road for another twenty minutes. After dropping off one man, a large crowd gathered around the vehicle and noticed me inside. A few of the men stood in front of the vehicle, preventing it from moving forward.

The situation did not make me nervous at first, but then a few of the men got into a heated argument over something as they were pointing to me and shouting at one another. The scene went from bad to worse very fast. I began to feel fear and thought I was about to become a victim of someone's hatred or greed — by either being hurt or killed by someone's weapon, or else having all of my belongings and money stolen.

All of the sudden as I looked up, there appeared to be what looked like a woman in a white Indian dress (a sari). Her head was covered and there was a light appearing on her, but I could not determine where the light was coming from because our car lights were pointing in another direction. She began to speak to the crowd of angry men, who stopped their arguing to listen to her. Then the men who were standing in front of the vehicle inexplicably stepped aside. Immediately, our driver hit the gas and drove off.

As we drove away, I looked back but could not see the woman at all. I realized immediately that this was an angel God had sent to protect me. I cried out in praise, thanking God for watching over me and delivering me safely to my destination.

Be encouraged and know I thank all of you for your prayers for us here desiring to see the kingdom of God advance. Please don't stop praying. Prayer is the most important tool, resource, and weapon that we have — far more than financial donations. Someone once asked which is more important in our mission work — prayer or funds — and I quickly responded, "If it's a choice between one's prayer or penny, I will always choose the prayer. Always!"

Praise be to the Lord Jesus Christ who protects, guides, sustains, and watches those of us who claim Him as Lord! He is our God, our Creator, Savior, and King! We worship our God in spirit and truth and don't bow to the idols made by the hands of people. We place our hope, trust, life, confidence, and faith in Him alone and believe He will reveal and show His love, grace, and compassion to anyone who seeks Him with a sincere and pure heart. Come, Lord Jesus!

The Bible says,

Make the Most High your dwelling—
*   even the LORD, who is my refuge—*
then no harm will befall you,
*   no disaster will come near your tent.*
For he will command his angels concerning you
*   to guard you in all your ways;*
they will lift you up in their hands,
*   so that you will not strike your foot against a stone."*
*   (Psalm 91:9-12)*

God is still doing miraculous things to cause His name to be known throughout the earth. Visions, healings, angelic encounters, demonic encounters, and supernatural events were not just for the book of Acts in the Bible. In many places in the world, it isn't hard to find someone who came to Jesus Christ by having a dream or vision or a miraculous healing. Many people ask me, "Why don't we see this more in America?" My answer is always, "I have no idea." Well, I do have some ideas, but I do not know the mind of God nor understand everything about how He works. No human being does.

Eastern culture is typically not based on the same kinds of intellectual and rational foundations so prevalent in the West. Belief in the supernatural is pervasive in most non-western cultures in the world. This includes the belief in witchcraft, evil spirits, and animism (which posits that spirits reside in objects). Although these beliefs are becoming more common in the West, they are still typically dismissed as irrational by most people. Perhaps God uses dreams, visions, and healings more often in other places around the world because He knows these approaches are especially crucial for such supernaturally minded people to come to faith in Jesus Christ. He may also do it simply because the people of these cultures are more open to these realities than we are in the West.

The Spirit of God does work in mysterious ways. Yet there are many issues around pneumatology (the study of the Holy Spirit) that are crucial for all followers of Jesus to understand if we are to live in victory, be empowered for ministry, and commune and grow with God.

MISUNDERSTANDING THE HOLY SPIRIT

The Holy Spirit is often misunderstood among many followers of Jesus. Here are a few wrong views of the Holy Spirit that I have heard people express:

The Holy Spirit exists only to punish me. Some may think that the Holy Spirit hunts down those who do wrong and "gets them." These people believe the Holy Spirit is like a cosmic policeman, whose sole function is to seek out those who are doing wrong and punish them. This is a wrong view of the Holy Spirit. Yes, the Holy Spirit convicts us of sin. In John 16:8-9, the Bible says, "When he comes, he will convict the world of guilt in regard to sin and righteousness and judgment." Yet the Holy Spirit does not exist just to *get you.*

The Holy Spirit exists to make me feel good. One of the most common mistakes Christians make about the Holy Spirit is in relation to our emotions. The Holy Spirit does not exist solely to make us feel good or fill us with "warm, fuzzy" feelings. He also comes to us to convict us of sin, bring salvation, and empower us for ministry. Emotion may at times be a by-product of the Holy Spirit's working in our lives, but it is not a prerequisite. It's true that life is filled with emotions, and frankly it would be a boring trip without them. But for Christians, emotions are not an end in themselves but should be seen as a tool God uses to transform our hearts, deepen our intimacy with Him, and produce fruit in our ministry to the world. The Holy Spirit will work through your emotions, but they do not have to be in any particular "state" for the Holy Spirit to do His work.

The Holy Spirit makes normal people abnormal. I have met some people who think they are more "spiritual" than others. Many times these "super-spiritual" people don't relate well with others. They convey a sense of superiority and arrogance toward the rest of us. Rather than listen to your story humbly and compassionately, they claim to know God's plan for your life and don't hesitate to tell you what it is. This is not a genuine effect of being filled with the Holy Spirit; rather, it is just another expression of the flesh, cloaked in a spiritual facade. As the saying goes, God does not want us to be so spiritually minded that we are no earthly good. The Holy Spirit empowers us to love people — humbly and compassionately — in practical ways.

The Holy Spirit is unknowable and scary. Some people fear the Holy Spirit. They picture him as a mystical "ghost" who haunts them, working behind the scenes of their lives in mysterious and frightening ways. I have met people who actually fear what the Holy Spirit would do to them if they gave their lives to God. But the apostle Paul says, "God did not give us a spirit of timidity, but a spirit of power, of love and of self-discipline" (2 Timothy 1:7). The Holy Spirit should not be feared but pursued with your whole heart. A. W. Tozer wrote, "The Spirit has will and intelligence and feeling and knowledge and sympathy and ability to love and see and think and hear and speak and desire as any person has."[1]

The Holy Spirit will work in my life only through a profound experience or encounter. Some Christians believe that every experience with the Holy Spirit must be very dramatic and strike them like lightning from the clouds. While this is a possibility, the Spirit often works in far more subtle and quiet ways. That is one reason why silence is such a great spiritual discipline, for very often we need solitude and quiet to be aware of the Spirit of God. The psalmist wrote,

> *"Be still, and know that I am God;*
> *I will be exalted among the nations,*
> *I will be exalted in the earth." (46:10)*

Consider some of the ways God speaks in silence: a flower in bloom, a sunset over the ocean, the conception of a baby in a woman, a seed taking root, and the greatest tribute of all to the Holy Spirit's "quiet" work, the resurrection of Jesus Christ from the dead.

UNDERSTANDING THE HOLY SPIRIT

Many volumes have been written to try to explain all the workings of the Holy Spirit. In this chapter, I will only scratch the surface. But I hope it will leave you hungry for more. Perhaps there is no other issue as divisive as the nature of the Holy Spirit and His role in the church. Yet there is nothing else that can unite the church besides the work of the Holy Spirit in a believer's life or in the church.

Since the early days of the church, the people of God have declared their belief and faith in the Holy Spirit. The Nicene Creed includes this: "I believe in the Holy Ghost, the Lord and Giver of life, which proceedeth from the Father and the Son, and with the Father and the Son together is worshiped and glorified."[2]

All through the Bible, there are references to the Holy Spirit's nature, personhood, and personality:

- "Where can I go from your Spirit? Where can I flee from your presence? If I go up to the heavens, you are there; if I make my bed in the depths, you are there." (Psalm 139:7-8)
- "Go and make disciples of all nations, baptizing them in the name of the Father and of the Son and of the Holy Spirit." (Matthew 28:19)
- "Flesh gives birth to flesh, but the Spirit gives birth to spirit." (John 3:6)
- "I will ask the Father, and he will give you another Counselor to be with you forever—the Spirit of truth. The world cannot accept him, because it neither sees him nor knows him. But you know him, for he lives with you and will be in you." (John 14:16-17)
- "If the Spirit of him who raised Jesus from the dead is living in you, he who raised Christ from the dead will also give life to your mortal bodies through his Spirit, who lives in you." (Romans 8:11)

The chief function of the Holy Spirit is to illumine Jesus' teaching, glorify His person, and work in the life of the individual believer and the church.[3] The work of the Holy Spirit is always to exalt Jesus Christ.

If you hear someone talking about the Holy Spirit in a way that does not put emphasis on Jesus Christ, be cautious. The Holy Spirit never exalts Himself but always works to magnify Jesus.

Because the Holy Spirit is the power by which believers come to Christ and become spiritually awakened, He is interwoven in our lives, dwelling in our heart and soul. Though we cannot see Him, we can be assured that He is at work in our individual lives and in the world. In the Old Testament, the Hebrew word used for the Spirit of God is *ruach*, meaning "breath," "wind," or "breeze."[4]

While living in Nepal, I heard a story of an untrained pastor who told his church that everyone in his village had the Holy Spirit. He had heard that the word *spirit* meant "breath" and went on to explain that if they held their hand in front of their mouths, they would feel the Holy Spirit coming out. Of course, this was incorrect teaching. The Holy Spirit is not the actual breath that comes out of your mouth.

The word for *Spirit* always used in the New Testament is *pneuma*, which means "wind or spirit."[5] In the New Testament, we find also the expressions "the Spirit of God," "the Spirit of the Lord," "the Spirit of the Father," "the Spirit of Jesus," and the "Spirit of Christ."

The Holy Spirit is the third person in the Trinity. He is fully God. He is eternal, omniscient (all knowing), and omnipresent (everywhere at all times); has a will; and can speak. He is alive. He is a person. He is not particularly visible in the Bible because His ministry is to bear witness of Jesus Christ.

HOW THE HOLY SPIRIT WORKS AND LEADS

The Christian life was not meant to be lived in isolation from the world. We are meant to practice missional habits and lifestyles that lead us to actively engage with people in all cultures. One of the dangers that has come from the rise of the Christian "subculture" in the West is the desire to withdraw from the lost and interact only with other

Christians. The word *mission* comes from the Latin word that means "to be sent." The word *mission* is not even in the Bible, but the theme is woven throughout. God sent His Son to the earth (see John 3:16). The Son sent the Spirit (see John 20:22). The triune God (Father, Son, and Holy Spirit) sends all of us into the world to proclaim the goodness and grace of God found in Jesus Christ. The Holy Spirit's work in our lives is key to understanding mission because it is the Holy Spirit who empowers us to live a life of mission, leading us to go boldly into the myriad cultures of the world to demonstrate and proclaim the love of Christ. Here is an overview of some of the primary ways the Holy Spirit works in and through our lives:

The Holy Spirit reveals God to us and empowers us to become like Christ. He reveals to Christians the deep things of God:

> *God has revealed it to us by his Spirit.*
> *The Spirit searches all things, even the deep things of God. For who among men knows the thoughts of a man except the man's spirit within him? In the same way no one knows the thoughts of God except the Spirit of God. We have not received the spirit of the world but the Spirit who is from God, that we may understand what God has freely given us. (1 Corinthians 2:10-12)*

In the same way, the Holy Spirit also reveals to us the mystery of Christ. As the apostle Paul explained,

> *The mystery [was] made known to me by revelation, as I have already written briefly. In reading this, then, you will be able to understand my insight into the mystery of Christ, which was not made known to men in other generations as it has now been revealed by the Spirit to God's holy apostles and prophets. (Ephesians 3:3-5)*

If we think we can become effective disciples of Jesus through our own willpower, we will surely be disappointed. The Holy Spirit works in our hearts to accomplish what we cannot do through our own ability, education, or determination. Though we must cooperate in the process, we are not the source of the transforming power; rather, it is His power, at work in our souls, that changes us into the image of Christ.

The soul is the inner life of a person, the seat of emotion, and the center of human personality. When we describe the soul, we often use words like *passion, desire, true self, life, living being, emotion,* and *longing.* Among other things, the Bible often describes the soul as the seat of desire or "the will." For example, we read about the desire for food (see Deuteronomy 12:20-21), the desire for love (see Song of Songs 1:7), the desire to long for God (see Psalm 63:1), the desire to rejoice (see Psalm 86:4), and the desire to know (see Psalm 139:14).

Whenever people are really being transformed into the likeness of Jesus, their desires, emotions, and passions change. Through the process of transformation, they leave behind their old life of selfishness, greed, and lust and take on more and more of Christ. This is the working of the Holy Spirit and not our own doing.

Are churches really producing people who are being transformed into the image of Jesus? Here is a little exercise to try, based on the fruit of the Spirit listed in Galatians 5:22-23 ("The fruit of the Spirit is love, joy, peace, patience, kindness, goodness, faithfulness, gentleness and self-control. Against such things there is no law."). Think of the typical churchgoers in your community and ask, "Are these people filled with love? Are they filled with joy?" Continue through the entire list. What do you notice as you examine the evidence? What about your own life? Are these the words that your best friend, spouse, or family member would use to describe you?

We don't have to scrutinize ourselves very much to realize that we all have a great deal of transforming to do. But to get there, we must adopt the same heart and attitude toward discipleship as the apostle Paul demonstrated when he wrote, "My dear children, for whom I am again in the pains of childbirth until Christ is formed in you" (Galatians 4:19). We have to surrender and submit to the Holy Spirit, who will work in us to remake us in the image of Christ.

The Holy Spirit helps us in our weakness. The Holy Spirit does in and through us what we cannot do by our own will or determination (see Colossians 1:29). This is the mystery of the Holy Spirit. Yielding to and trusting the work of the Holy Spirit is critical in our Christian journey. The Spirit enables us to pray and works through us. He discloses to us our needs and wants as well as our sins and shortcomings so as to impress upon us a deep sense of our absolute dependence on God: "In the same way, the Spirit helps us in our weakness. We do not know what we ought to pray for, but the Spirit himself intercedes for us with groans that words cannot express" (Romans 8:26).

We are often not aware of our wants, and we have no deep desire for those supplies of grace that we really need. We are led to say with the Laodiceans, "I am rich; I have acquired wealth and do not need a thing," not knowing that we "are wretched, pitiful, poor, blind and naked" (Revelation 3:17). During our times of weakness, it is absolutely crucial to pray that the Holy Spirit will fill us and empower us with His supernatural presence. A theme presented throughout Scripture is that we *have not* because we do not ask in faith (see James 1:6-7; 4:2; 1 John 3:22; 5:14).

The Holy Spirit empowers us to overcome the demonic and evil. While ministering in India one year, I lived at a local Bible college in Calcutta for several weeks. I enjoyed dining with, worshiping alongside, and getting to know all the students who came there from different parts of India. We had fun as well and would sneak up on the roof to trap pigeons for a late-night snack (grilled pigeon is actually not that bad). One day, I was asked to go along with the students as they went out to do evangelistic outreach in the streets of Calcutta. I immediately agreed. It was a beautiful sight to see Indians preaching the gospel to other Indians and passing out food and clothes. At one point, the students asked me to preach to the crowd that they had gathered.

I began to tell the crowd that, although I came from a different country, I was no different from them. I told them that I needed God and needed forgivness of sin. After two or three minutes of preaching through an interpreter, I noticed that an Indian man standing next to my interpreter would begin to talk loudly whenever the interpreter spoke. The faces in the crowd looked confused; they did not know who to listen to, my interpreter or the other man. At first I thought this man must be drunk, but after a little observation, I could tell he was not. I began to sense an evil spirit from this man and realized that he was keeping the crowd from hearing the gospel.

Without hesitation, I looked directly at him and said, "In the name of Jesus Christ, I command you to leave this place and to stop preventing these people from hearing about Jesus." Immediately the man walked away. The people saw this and were amazed. Honestly, so was I. The crowd grew as more and more gathered to hear about Jesus. The incident was an incredible reminder of the reality of evil forces in the world and their efforts to keep people from hearing about Jesus Christ.

Christians tend to take one of two extremes when it comes to the issue of evil and demonic influence. They either emphasize the Devil too much or they don't focus enough on the reality of evil. The Christian's true place of strength rests in the middle ground between these two extremes. Paul admonished the believers in Ephesus,

Put on the full armor of God so that you can take your stand against the devil's schemes. For our struggle is not against flesh and blood, but against the rulers, against the authorities, against the powers of this dark world and against the spiritual forces of evil in the heavenly realms." (Ephesians 6:11-12)

During His ministry, Jesus referred to the Spirit of God as the power by which He cast out demons, thereby invading the stronghold of Satan and freeing those held captive (see Matthew 12:28-29; Luke 11:20). In the same way, the Spirit works with the Father and Son in releasing the redeeming power of the kingdom of God through us.[6]

So many people try to minister solely through their own strength — that is, their own ability, personality, and talents. Certainly, God has blessed each of us with unique natural gifts and personalities. God gifted Billy Graham differently from Mother Teresa. Whatever our natural gifts, however, we must surrender them to God and allow the Holy Spirit to equip us with His supernatural life and ministry. Only then will we have lasting fruit and be able to face evil in whatever form it takes.

While many in the Christian family will continue to argue about exactly how evil manifests itself in the world, no follower of Jesus can deny that the Enemy is alive and active. Whether evil manifests through an individual (such as Adolph Hitler, Pol Pot of Cambodia, or Saddam Hussein of Iraq) or in a more systemic way (through governments, organizations, or companies), we must seek the wisdom of the Holy Spirit to guide our actions, words, and steps so that the gospel of Jesus Christ is free to bring sight to the spiritually blind and freedom to those in spiritual prison.

Another time while ministering in India, I found myself on the streets sharing Christ with my Indian friends. After a long day of preaching the gospel, distributing food, and praying for the sick, I experienced an amazing encounter that I will never forget. After a team of us had been in a park playing a guitar and sharing about Jesus Christ for an hour, I looked down and saw a man who had legs as round as a pipe sitting at my feet. He could not walk and looked as if he lived on the streets. He was pulling at my pant legs to get my attention. At first I did not know what he wanted or what he was trying to tell me. But then he began to point at his deformed legs, then up to the

Ministering on the Streets in India

Bible I was holding in my hand, and then up at the sky. He did this about five times before I realized what he was trying to say: "If your God is powerful, have Him fix my legs."

I was overwhelmed with compassion. I was convinced that God was going to heal this man before the crowd of fifty or so Hindus who had been listening to us preach about Christ. Our small team gathered around the man and began to pray fervently for him to be healed in the name of Jesus Christ so all the people could see the power of the gospel demonstrated. After praying, nothing happened. I left feeling so discouraged and defeated.

Why, God? I asked. *We have been preaching all day and sharing about Christ all over the city of Calcutta, and we prayed in faith that you would heal that man. Why didn't You? It would've been such a powerful testimony.*

After wrestling with God over this, I heard His still small voice in my soul: "I want you to be faithful in preaching the gospel and praying for the sick. You are not called to be successful, only faithful. Be faithful."

It is a lesson I still remember to this day. As followers of Christ, we are called to be faithful and obedient to whatever God leads us to do. That's all. The results are up to God. Paul wrote, "The Lord is faithful, and he will strengthen and protect you from the evil one. We have confidence in the Lord that you are doing and will continue to do the things we command. May the Lord direct your hearts into God's love and Christ's perseverance" (2 Thessalonians 3:3-5).

The Holy Spirit empowers us to speak the gospel with courage and clarity. In Acts 4:31, we read, "And they were all filled with the Holy Spirit and spoke the word of God boldly." More than ever, I believe we need the filling of the Holy Spirit to articulate the good news of Jesus with grace and love. Jesus Christ alone can bring salvation, meaning, identity, security, and eternal life to people's hearts. We offer hope to the lonely, broken, and rejected. Jesus Christ is this hope. May the Holy Spirit empower us to have conversations with our friends and family that inspire them to seek to know Jesus for themselves.

The Holy Spirit gives us dreams and visions for our lives. Vision makes people come alive. The Holy Spirit releases life-giving visions and dreams in God's people. When you hear someone cast a vision in the Spirit, it truly does something powerful and inspirational for those who hear. We all want vision — vision for our life, marriage, church, work, and ministry. As the proverb says, "Where there is no vision, the people perish" (29:18, KJV).

I think vision is simply seeing what *can* become reality and not being stuck in what exists *now*. It is seeing the potential in someone else, an organization, a country, a church, or a company. People with little vision seem incapable of seeing anything beyond the here and now. But those with vision see what is possible. It's the difference between the "real" and the "ideal." What is the current reality and what is the ideal reality we can move toward? Regardless of whether it is a pastor sharing a vision for a church, a presidential candidate sharing vision for a nation, or a teacher sharing vision to a classroom of children, we all need to see not only what is but also what can be. We need to know not only who we are right now but also, through God's power, who we can become. God said,

> *"I will pour out my Spirit on all people.*
> *Your sons and daughters will prophesy,*
> *your old men will dream dreams,*
> *your young men will see visions." (Joel 2:28)*

We need more dreamers and visionaries. Those who can articulate with clarity God's vision for His people are much needed. One stumbling block of the church is its stubborn desire for the mundane and predictable. We want worship music that always sounds the same, sermons that all sound alike, and people who talk like everyone else.

There is lack of vision in the missionary enterprise as well. We need Spirit-led authenticity and uniqueness in our dreams and visions for reaching a world for Jesus Christ. There's a great need for entrepreneurial missionaries who can pioneer innovative ministries and churches around the world.

When I first started ServLife, many people did not understand what I was doing. Actually, some people still do not understand. For every one person who is excited and supportive of my work, there are three who do not get it and respond with confusion or skepticism. Many people over the years have expressed concern over why I did not simply join an existing ministry or missionary organization. One gentleman asked me, "Why did you start your own organization? Isn't that just reinventing the wheel?"

I responded, "I sure hope so."

He just looked at me, obviously puzzled.

I believe there are many reading this book who have a dream for a ministry, business, nation, or people group. My encouragement to you is this: GO FOR IT! Do not let anyone or anything stop you from letting God see your dream become a reality. Yes, seek counsel and advice from others. As Proverbs 15:22 says, "Plans fail for lack of counsel, but with many advisers they succeed." Yes, people will discourage you—probably the ones you least expect to. Many will offer little encouragement or support. Money may be short, but if God calls you, who can stop you?

Perhaps you are having trouble identifying your calling. The author Frederick Buechner gave a wonderful bit of wisdom about finding your unique purpose when he wrote, "Your calling is where your greatest joys and the world's greatest needs intersect." When do you most feel alive? When is it that you experience the deepest sense of joy in what you are doing? Perhaps it is with children. Perhaps it's when you are in the mountains. Perhaps it's in another culture. Whatever it is, ask God to pour out His Spirit and reveal to you how your passion can be used for His glory.

God wants to give you purpose even more than you desire to receive it. Here are some suggestions on how you can begin to dream:

- Research cities and countries throughout the world that are less than 5 percent Christian. Dream about what it would take for that city or nation to become 20 percent Christian. What would be needed? What could you do to help inspire a change like that? How could you give your life to such a great cause?
- It's estimated that every day about thirty thousand people die from preventable diseases, such as pneumonia, tuberculosis, measles, and diarrhea. How could you spend your life getting this number reduced or even eliminated?
- Nine to ten thousand Nepalese girls, most between the ages of nine and sixteen, are drawn into the sex traffic industry in India every year.[7] How could you change this? What could you

do with your life to stop this tragedy?

- Cambodia suffers from an infant mortality rate of 135 deaths per one thousand births. Compare this to the infant mortality rate of America, which is 1.2 deaths per one thousand births. How might you help to reduce the infant mortality rate in Cambodia?

In 1806, a small group of students at Williams College gathered outside to pray. As they prayed, a rainstorm hit, forcing the five students to run to a nearby haystack to keep dry. Once there, they continued to pray, and the Holy Spirit began to place a vision in their hearts. They committed themselves as a group "to send the gospel to the pagans of Asia, and to the disciples of Mohammed." By 1810, they had inspired the Congregationalists of Massachusetts and Connecticut to organize the American Board of Commissioners of Foreign Missions, America's first foreign missionary society. The famous missionaries Adoniram Judson and Luther Rice were a part of that first group of missionaries who were sent out from America in 1812. All of this came from a vision received by a group of students huddled by a haystack in the pouring rain.[8]

The Holy Spirit inspires our creativity. The work of the Holy Spirit in our lives allows us all to be artists. Through the Spirit, we all have the capacity to create beauty and inspire others in a thousand different ways. Many people will say, "I am not an artist." But I would argue that we are all artists in Christ, for His Spirit empowers us all to create beauty through all we do.

Now, we may not be able to earn a salary with what we create, as some can, but we can use our creativity to offer hope and encouragement to others, or even inspire them to action. It may be through a simple greeting card you make yourself, a photograph you take, or a poem you write. Or perhaps your creativity lies in cooking, singing, teaching children, repairing cars, or throwing parties. But whatever your creative bent, God can take what you have and make it something beautiful and inspiring for others.

There is a great need for a revolution of creativity in the body of Christ. I believe that people who do not know God are drawn to "holy creativity." When they see people who create out of love rather than merely for profit or recognition, they will be inspired to seek out the source of that love which is Jesus Himself.

We as a mission organization are trying to empower and unleash artists within the body of Christ to help bring awareness and education to the body of Christ about global issues. One young man in the Midwest was determined to inspire children through photography. He wrote our office and asked for a small amount of start-up capital so he could buy a few dozen disposable cameras. He spent a whole day teaching a group of several dozen children how to take photographs. They walked through the parks and streets taking photographs of interesting things they saw. They took photographs of other children as well. A week later, he organized a public photo exhibit of each child's two best photos. The proceeds from the sale of the photographs (mostly bought by the parents) were sent to our mission to support the work we do among orphanages. While teaching the children to be creative, he also educated them about needs around the world.

The Holy Spirit guides us in prayer. Oftentimes when we do not see fruit in ministry, it is because we are not praying right. I heard Peter Wagner tell a great story at Fuller Seminary on the need for strategic prayer. Iraq invaded Kuwait in 1991 and later fired scud missiles into Israel. It is commonly known that the only way Saddam Hussein could find out where his scud missiles landed was by watching CNN. On the other hand, American bombs were known as "smart bombs." They were guided to their specific targets by a sophisticated laser targeting system. I've heard it said that you can make a smart bomb fly hundreds of miles and land right on top of a dime, provided the laser is pointed at that dime. Some Christians' prayers are like scud missiles. We just fire off ambiguous requests to God, hoping they will make a difference but never really knowing whether they have any effect. On the other hand, some Christians know the power of guided, strategic prayers that make the demons of hell shake in their boots.

The Bible says,

> For though we live in the world, we do not wage war as the world does. The weapons we fight with are not the weapons of the world. On the contrary, they have divine power to demolish strongholds. We demolish arguments and every pretension that sets itself up against the knowledge of God, and we take captive every thought to make it obedient to Christ. (2 Corinthians 10:3-6)

We must learn to wage war, not in an aimless way but with specific and guided prayers, allowing the Holy Spirit to guide us.

GUIDELINES FOR STRATEGIC PRAYER

Here are a few guidelines to help you pray strategically in the Holy Spirit:

Pray with other people. We should not wage war alone. Satan and all his demons are scared to death when followers of Jesus gather to pray. They could not care less if we just got together to eat, talk, and laugh. But when we gather to pray together and agree with each other in prayer, watch out. Jesus said, "I tell you that if two of you on earth agree about anything you ask for, it will be done for you by my Father in heaven. For where two or three come together in my name, there am I with them" (Matthew 18:19-20).

When you gather with others to pray, it is helpful to remind your group about the power of agreement. Whenever someone is praying, encourage others in the group to say aloud, "I agree," "Yes," or "Amen" (which simply means "so be it"). You don't have to shout this or be

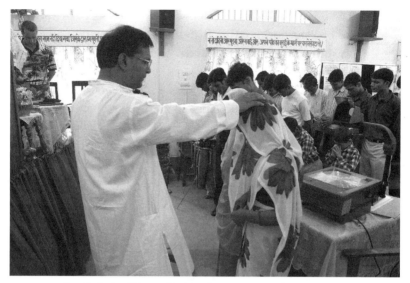

ServLife Staff Prays for Hindu Woman Seeking Healing

disruptive, but speak loudly enough so that the one who is praying knows you are agreeing with his or her prayer to God.

When confronted with evil, talk to Jesus first. When you come across evil in your own life or in someone else's life, you should pray to Jesus first and not try to address the demonic force directly. Allow Jesus Christ to be the center of your thoughts and begin to worship and focus on His greatness. Ask Him to guide you and lead you in what you should do. Perhaps sing a song you know that brings Jesus to the center. The darkness does not like the light. And when the light of Christ is brought before our minds and hearts, there is power there. Jesus Christ defeated Satan at the cross and at the resurrection. This is where Scripture memorization is vital. When you sense the presence of evil in your own heart or in the heart of someone around you, begin to speak Scripture that you have memorized. A few passages to start with are:

- "You, dear children, are from God and have overcome them, because the one who is in you is greater than the one who is in the world." (1 John 4:4)

- "They overcame him by the blood of the Lamb and by the word of their testimony; they did not love their lives so much as to shrink from death." (Revelation 12:11)
- "The weapons we fight with are not the weapons of the world. On the contrary, they have divine power to demolish strongholds. We demolish arguments and every pretension that sets itself up against the knowledge of God, and we take captive every thought to make it obedient to Christ." (2 Corinthians 10:4-5)

And as you confront evil, always remember: Jesus has the ultimate power over evil and is our greatest weapon against it.

When you pray for someone who does not know God, ask the Holy Spirit to open his or her eyes to see. The Bible says, "The god of this age [Satan] has blinded the minds of unbelievers, so that they cannot see the light of the gospel of the glory of Christ, who is the image of God" (2 Corinthians 4:4). When we have friends and family members who do not know or love God, we must learn to pray that the blindfolds Satan has placed over their eyes will be removed. We must pray specific prayers in order to see specific change. This same principle applies as we pray for whole cities and nations as well.

LET JUSTICE ROLL

With all my heart, I want to see people offer their lives, gifts, ambitions, and vocations to the expansion of God's global kingdom. Many parts of the world are so often forgotten—so desperately in need of hope and relief. My prayer is for a never-ending stream of workers to flow in and eradicate injustice, end hunger, and multiply the church for God's glory and renown. I love the words of the Old Testament prophet Amos, "But let justice roll on like a river, righteousness like a never-failing stream!" (5:24). May the Spirit of God move in the hearts, imaginations, and lives of His people like never before.

FOR REFLECTION AND DISCUSSION

1. How might the Holy Spirit use your creativity to bless others?

2. Have you ever heard teaching on the Holy Spirit that was not accurate? What was it? How did you determine that it wasn't the truth?

3. Have you ever heard someone share a dream inspired by the Holy Spirit? If so, what was it?

4. What dreams do you believe the Holy Spirit is leading you to pursue? If you can't think of one, what sort of dream would you really love the Holy Spirit to give you for your life?

5. What's one thing you deeply desire for your life — something that you know will take the power of the Holy Spirit to accomplish? What do you think God is saying to you about that desire?

NOTES

CHAPTER 1

1. David B. Barrett, George T. Kurian, and Todd M. Johnson, eds., *World Christian Encyclopedia: A Comparative Survey of Churches and Religions in The Modern World*, 2nd ed. (New York: Oxford University Press, 2001), 19, 551.
2. Barrett, Kurian, and Johnson, 405.
3. Barrett, Kurian, and Johnson, 532.
4. James F. Engel and William A. Dyrness, *Changing the Mind of Missions: Where Have We Gone Wrong?* (Downers Grove, IL: InterVarsity, 2000), 18.
5. Merriam-Webster's Collegiate Dictionary, 11th ed., s.v. "paradox."
6. *Biblesoft's New Exhaustive Strong's Numbers and Concordance with Expanded Greek-Hebrew Dictionary.* CD-ROM. Biblesoft and International Bible Translators, 1994, s.v. "sundoulos."
7. Norimitsu Onishi, "Faith and Values: Korean Export—Salvation," *New York Times*, November 27, 2004.
8. Dallas Willard, (lecture, Renovare Conference, Houston, TX, 1998).
9. Engel and Dyrness, 22.
10. Brian D. McLaren, *A New Kind of Christian* (San Francisco: Jossey-Bass, 2001), 29.

11. Rick Warren, *The Purpose-Driven Life* (Grand Rapids, MI: Zondervan, 2002), 171.

12. Gordon Cosby quoted in Jeff Bailey, "The Journey Inward, Outward, and Forward," Vineyard USA, Cutting Edge Newsletter, Fall 2001.

13. *Biblesoft's New Exhaustive*, s.v. "ecclesia."

CHAPTER 2

1. Lesslie Newbigin, *The Gospel in a Pluralistic Society* (Grand Rapids, MI.: Eerdmans, 1989), 18.

CHAPTER 3

1. James F. Engel and William A. Dyrness, *Changing the Mind of Missions: Where Have We Gone Wrong?* (Downers Grove, IL: InterVarsity, 2000), 160.

2. Matthew Henry, *Matthew Henry's Commentary on the Whole Bible: New Modern Edition*, electronic database (Hendrickson Publishers, 1991).

3. Author unknown.

CHAPTER 4

1. Ranjit Chaudhuri, "*Towards Understanding Gandhian Economics*," Essays on Gandhian Thought (Institute of Gandhian Studies, Wardha), http://www.mkgandhi.org/articles/Eco_ranjit.htm.

2. John Caputo, *On Religion: Thinking in Action* (New York: Routledge, 2001), 2.

3. Ron Blue, "Generous Living: Finding Contentment Through Giving" (speech, Generous Giving Conference, Atlanta, GA, January 15, 1999).

4. Bill Bright quoted in Ron Blue, *Generous Living: Finding Contentment Through Giving* (Grand Rapids, MI: Zondervan, 1997), 201.

5. George Barna, *Barna Research Archives: Money* (Barna Research Group).

6. Ralph Winter, *Missions Frontiers*, "Student Debt and Missionary Service," July–August 2004, 4.

7. George Barna, *How to Increase Giving in Your Church: A Practical Guide to the Sensitive Task of Raising Money for Your Church or Ministry* (Ventura, CA: Regal, 1997), 20.

8. Gandhi quoted at http://www.quotiki.com/quote.aspx?id=5167.

9. Scott Lewis, "Choosing to Give the Rest to the Lord: My Journey of Faith," "Stories and Testimonies," "Generous Giving," http://www.generousgiving.org/articles/display .asp?id=3. For ideas and resources for giving, visit www.generousgiving.com.

CHAPTER 5

1. William Jay Jacobs, *Mother Teresa: Helping the Poor*, revised ed. (Brookfield, CT: Millbrook, 1998), 2–4.

2. A. W. Tozer quoted in Erik Segalini "Come In," Worldwide Challenge (Campus Crusade for Christ), July–August 1997, vol. 24, no. 4, http://www.worldwidechallenge.org/1997/ comein.html.

3. Søren Kierkegaard quoted in Greg Cole, "Lord, Teach Us to Pray" (sermon given at Emmanuel Church, Newport, RI, July 25, 2004), http://www.emmanuelnewport.org/rector72504 .htm.

4. C. S. Lewis quoted at http://thinkexist.com/quotation/god _whispers_to_us_in_our_pleasures-speaks_to_us/180233. html.

5. Meister Eckhart quoted in J. Heinrich Arnold, *Discipleship: Living for Christ in the Daily Grind* (Farmington, PN: Plough Publishing, 1991), 24.

CHAPTER 6

1. Rit Nosotro, "James Hudson Taylor," Hyperhistory.net, http://www.hyperhistory.net/apwh/bios/b3hudsoneu.htm.
2. Ray C. Stedman, "It All Depends on Me," (Discovery Publishing, 1968), http://www.raystedman.org/genesis/3663.html.
3. Ken Curtis, Beth Jacobson, Diana Severance, Ann T. Snyder, and Dan Graves, *Glimpses* (Worcester, PA: Christian History Institute, 1991).
4. *The Wall Street Journal Europe*, March 14, 2003.
5. David B. Barrett and Todd M. Johnson, *World Christian Trends AD 30–AD 2000: Interpreting the Annual Christian Megacensus* (Pasadena, CA: William Carey Library, 2001), 34.
6. Barrett and Johnson, 551.
7. *Biblesoft's New Exhaustive Strong's Numbers and Concordance with Expanded Greek-Hebrew Dictionary*. CD-ROM. Biblesoft and International Bible Translators, 1994, s.v. "splagchnizomai."
8. Ken Curtis and Diana Severance, *Glimpses* (Worcester, PA Christian History Institute, 1991).

CHAPTER 7

1. Elisabeth Elliot, *Shadow of the Almighty: The Life and Testament of Jim Elliot* (New York: Harper & Row, 1958).
2. *Biblesoft's New Exhaustive Strong's Numbers and Concordance with Expanded Greek-Hebrew Dictionary*. CD-ROM. Biblesoft and International Bible Translators, 1994, s.v. "martus."
3. John Foxe, *Foxe's Book of Martyrs*, entry regarding the death of James.
4. David B. Barrett, George T. Kurian, and Todd M. Johnson, eds., *World Christian Encyclopedia: A Comparative Survey of Churches and Religions in the Modern World,* 2nd ed. (New York: Oxford University Press, 2001).

5. http://www.state.gov.

6. http://www.persecutedchurch.org.

7. Correspondence reprinted by permission of the author.

CHAPTER 8

1. Gary Haugen, *Good News About Injustice: A Witness of Courage in a Hurting World* (Downers Grove, IL: InterVarsity, 1999), 45.

2. David J. Bosch, *Transforming Mission: Paradigm Shifts in Theology of Mission* (Maryknoll, NY: Orbis, 1996), 508.

3. "Human Trafficking: Introduction," The World Revolution, http://www.worldrevolution.org/guidepage/humantrafficking/intro.

4. "Human Trafficking: Human Trafficking Facts," The World Revolution, http://www.worldrevolution.org/Projects/Webguide/GuideArticle.asp?ID=1421.

5. http://www.state.gov.

6. Under Secretary of State for Global Affairs Paula J. Dobriansky, speech, Stop Child Trafficking: Modern-Day Slavery conference, Helsinki, Finland, June 2003.

7. Penelope Saunders, "Sexual Trafficking and Forced Prostitution of Children," October 29, 1998.

8. Global March Against Child Labour, "Report on the Worst Forms of Child Labour," http://www.globalmarch.org/resourcecentre/world/nepal.pdf.

9. Saunders, "Sexual Trafficking."

10. United Nation's Office of High Commissioner of Human Rights, "Fact Sheet No. 14, Contemporary Forms of Slavery."

11. Human Rights Watch, "Children's Rights: Child Labor," http://hrw.org/children/labor.htm.

12. Human Rights Watch, "The Small Hands of Slavery," http://www.hrw.org/reports/1996/India3.htm.

13. *Adam Clarke's Commentary.* CD-ROM. Biblesoft and International Bible Translators, 1996.

14. The World Revolution, "The State of the World: A Brief Introduction to Global Issues," http://www.worldrevolution .org/projects/globalissuesoverview/overview2/BriefOverview .htm.

15. The World Revolution, "The State of the World."

16. Oxfam, "Education for All: A Compact for Africa," http:// www.oxfam.org.uk/what_we_do/issues/education/education _africa.htm.

17. Oxfam, "Education for All."

18. Crispin Hughes, OxfamAmerica, "Global Health Crisis," http://www.oxfamamerica.org/whatwedo/issues_we_work_on/ trade/news_publications/trips/art5386.html.

19. The World Revolution, "The State of the World."

20. World Health Organization, Regional Office for Africa, Division of Healthy Environments and Sustainable Development, Food Safety Unit (FOS), "Hand Washing and Food Safety," http://www.afro.who.int/des/fos/afro_codex-fact-sheets/handwash-fact-sheet2.pdf.

21. World Bank, "Global Poverty Measures 1987-1998 and Projections for the Future," 1999.

22. United Nations Human Development: Human Development Report, 1999.

23. World Development Movement. Rebecca McQullan, World Development Movement, WDM in Action, Winter 1999, cited in The World Revolution, "Overview of Global Issues: Development and Poverty," http://www.worldrevolution.org/ projects/globalissuesoverview/overview2/BriefPeace.htm.

24. United Nations Development Program: Human Development Report 1998.

25. United Nations Development Program: Human Development Report 1997.

26. http://www.homelandonline.org.
27. http://www.tibetanphotoproject.com.
28. John Waters, *David Livingstone: Apostle to Africa* (Bombay, India: Gospel Literature Service, 1992), 13.

CHAPTER 9
1. Jarrett Richardson, "Psychopathology in Missionary Personnel," in Kelly O'Donnell, ed. (Pasadena, CA: William Carey Library, 1992), 97.
2. Richard Swenson, *A Minute of Margin* (Colorado Springs: NavPress, 2003), reading 33.
3. http://www.uc.edu/news/ebriefs/yawn.htm.

CHAPTER 10
1. A. W. Tozer, *Being Filled with the Holy Spirit* (Camp Hill, PA: Christian Publications, 1972), 24.
2. The Nicene Creed, http://www.creeds.net/ancient/nicene.htm.
3. *Nelson's Illustrated Bible Dictionary* (Thomas Nelson Publishers, 1986).
4. *International Standard Bible Encyclopedia.* CD-ROM. Biblesoft and International Bible Translators, 1996.
5. *New American Standard Updated Edition Exhaustive Concordance of the Bible with Hebrew-Aramaic and Greek Dictionaries* (La Habra, CA: The Lockman Foundation, 1998), s.v. "pneuma."
6. *Nelson's Illustrated Bible Dictionary.*
7. Global March Against Child Labour, "Report on the Worst Forms of Child Labour," http://www.globalmarch.org/resourcecentre/world/nepal.pdf.
8. Ken Curtis, Beth Jacobson, Diana Severance, Ann T. Snyder, and Dan Graves, *Glimpses* (Worcester, PA: Christian History Institute, 2003).

ABOUT SERVLIFE INTERNATIONAL, INC.

Joel Vestal started ServLife while a nineteen-year-old college student at Baylor University. As a result of walking through the streets of Calcutta, the hospitals of Baghdad, the villages of southeast Africa, the jungles of Indonesia, war-torn Sudan, the slums of Cairo, the deserts of Algeria, and oppressed Cuba, it was obvious that an army of indigenous missionaries were eager to evangelize and empower their own people but lacked training, encouragement, and support. Thus, ServLife was established.

ServLife seeks to build global community by creating mission communities (teams) among the most marginalized and oppressed regions of the world to rescue and care for at-risk children, to end hunger, and to train/multiply the indigenous church to advance the whole gospel to the whole person.

Please visit our website at www.servlife.org to learn more about our efforts and explore ways you can get involved.

ABOUT THE AUTHOR

Joel Vestal is a native of Texas. He did his undergraduate work at Baylor University and graduate work at Fuller Seminary in California. Joel has spoken at numerous organizations, churches, universities, and seminaries. He served on the board of WorldconneX, a missions ministry of the Baptist General Convention of Texas, and has traveled to more than seventy nations.

Joel has had numerous international adventures (some of which you read in this book): He met Mother Teresa on several occasions and was on national television in Iraq, interrogated by secret police in Cuba, in the middle of civil war in Sudan, and part of a team that started the first Christian church in a city in north India. Joel and Elise are proud parents of Zayd and Daya. Currently, the Vestals make their home in Indianapolis. The names of their children give the mission of the Vestal family: "to increase in compassion" (*Zayd*—Arabic, meaning "to increase"; *Daya*—Hindi, meaning "compassion").

CHECK OUT THESE OTHER GREAT TITLES FROM NAVPRESS!

Daughters of Eve

Virginia Stem Owens
ISBN-13: 978-1-60006-200-1
ISBN-10: 1-60006-200-8
Virginia Stem Owens invites you to examine some of the fasci-
nating stories of biblical women. Many of the issues they faced
(violence, multiple marriages, manipulation, motherhood) are
issues of urgent importance to women today. Much has changed since the first
woman walked the earth, but at least one thing remains the same: Being a
woman is as challenging as it ever was.

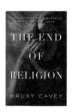

The End of Religion

Bruxy Cavey
ISBN-13: 978-1-60006-067-0
ISBN-10: 1-60006-067-6
Throughout the history of our world, religion has been a con-
tentious concept. But what if God himself has no interest in
religion? Author Bruxy Cavey asserts that Christ came to earth to
end religion in favor of relationship. Seekers will discover the wondrous promise
found in our Savior, and believers will hear anew Christ's call to walk in love
and freedom.

The Year I Got Everything I Wanted

Cameron Conant
ISBN-13: 978-1-60006-145-5
ISBN-10: 1-60006-145-1
Cameron Conant was on the verge of a new life full of promise.
After a painful divorce, he set out to pursue a new job oppor-
tunity and a promising relationship. But just one year later,
Cameron was unemployed and reeling from two failed relationships. *The Year I
Got Everything I Wanted* provides a fresh parallel to the book of Ecclesiastes, as
Cameron searches for meaning and purpose.

Visit your local bookstore, call NavPress at 1-800-366-7788, or log on to
www.navpress.com to purchase.

Environmental Benefits Statement

Active, holistic faith is the backbone of NavPress Deliberate books. We believe that every decision impacts the world of which God has charged us to be good stewards. We are good stewards when we care for people — from choosing to befriend a difficult next-door neighbor to volunteering at a homeless shelter. We are good stewards of the rest of creation by consuming resources wisely and in a way that also renews and blesses the world, its creatures, and its people. We believe in practicing what we publish, so all NavPress Deliberate books are "green." We have chosen to use paper products that do not contribute to deforestation in the world's poorest nations but instead reuse the waste produced by our own consumer culture. The chart below shows the positive impact this decision has on our environment this year.

	UNRECYCLED PAPER	DELIBERATE PAPER	DIFFERENCE
Wood Use	52 tons	26 tons	26 tons
Total Energy	575 million BTU's	450 million BTU's	125 million BTU's
Greenhouse Gases	85,353 lbs CO_2 equiv.	69,542 lbs CO_2 equiv.	15,811 lbs CO_2 equiv.
Wastewater	286,128 gallons	220,501 gallons	65,627 gallons
Solid Waste	34,175 pounds	25,748 pounds	8,427 pounds